WITHDRAWN

Illinois Central College
Learning Resources Center

THE EMPTY POLLING BOOTH

THE EMPTY POLLING BOOTH

Arthur T. Hadley

(with data developed by Frederick T. Steeper and additional research by Felicity V. Swayze)

PRENTICE-HALL, INC. / *Englewood Cliffs, N.J.*

JK
1987
.H33

The Empty Polling Booth by Arthur T. Hadley
Copyright © 1978 by Arthur T. Hadley
All rights reserved. No part of this book may be
reproduced in any form or by any means, except
for the inclusion of brief quotations in a review,
without permission in writing from the publisher.
Printed in the United States of America
Prentice-Hall International, Inc., London
Prentice-Hall of Australia, Pty. Ltd., Sydney
Prentice-Hall of Canada, Ltd., Toronto
Prentice-Hall of India Private Ltd., New Delhi
Prentice-Hall of Japan, Inc., Tokyo
Prentice-Hall of Southeast Asia Pte. Ltd., Singapore
Whitehall Books Limited, Wellington, New Zealand
10 9 8 7 6 5 4 3 2 1

Library of Congress Cataloging in Publication Data
Hadley, Arthur Twining
    The empty polling booth.

    Bibliography: p.
    Includes index.
    1. Voting—United States—Abstention.   I. Steeper,
Frederick T., joint author.   II. Swayze, Felicity V.,
joint author.   III. Title.
JK1987.H33   324'.2   78-16966
ISBN 0-13-274928-9

This book is dedicated to the 2,006 Americans, voters and refrainers who permitted themselves to be interviewed for our survey, particularly those who graciously gave of their time to be reinterviewed at length. Quite literally, this book could not have been done without you, and I thank you all.

CONTENTS

INTRODUCTION

I first met Robert Teeter in the confused political summer of 1973, about a year before the departure of Richard Nixon from the White House. I was writing a book on what the potential Presidential candidates were doing outside the spotlight of press coverage in the three years before the New Hampshire primary. Teeter, the Executive Vice-President of Market Opinion Research of Detroit, Michigan, was polling for the Republican party. The reports he was producing on the American voter were admired by both academia and the press. The two of us discovered that we shared an interest and a belief: an interest in the ever-growing numbers of people who did *not* vote, and a belief that these people constituted the major political reality—and problem—of the 1970's. To both of us it seemed incredible that so little was known about nonvoters beyond one astounding fact: *that they were 65 million in numbers, or nearly 46 percent of all Americans of voting age.*

Our common enthusiasm drew us into friendship, and I asked Teeter if he would do a poll, after the 1976 election, make the data available to me, and help me to analyze them so that I could write a book on who was not voting—and why. He was able to persuade Market Opinion Research to do this and they most generously supplied me with the data he gathered. Beginning the night of President Carter's election, November 2, 1976, Market Opinion Research polled a random sample of 2,006 citizens eligible to vote. Together, separately, and with the generous help of others, we studied and organized the data. Later I reinterviewed in depth some 100 of our previous interviewees. At the same time I researched the history and theory of voting and not voting both in America and abroad. That Teeter is a Republican and I am a Democrat is important. While I alone am responsible for the final organization of nonvoters into categories and for the conclusions of this book, we both hope that its bipartisan foundations will help people accept its findings and recommendations.

In stressing my sole responsibility for the organization and conclusions of this book I am not trying to take an undue share of the credit. Far from it. Market Opinion Research and Robert Teeter were indispensable. But they should not be held responsible for my conclusions, errors, or style. This book is directed to all those who are interested in voting and not voting, who care about the state of American politics today. Were this a purely academic work, it would have a more tentative tone. The native hue of its resolution would be sicklied o'er with the pale cast of footnote.

How is the book organized?

The first chapter begins with an examination of the present rise in nonvoting, and discusses why this rise is important, even alarming. Then the contradictions between our data and the traditional stereotype of the nonvoter are laid bare. Finally the chapter examines the general concepts that we found distinguished voter from nonvoter and it briefly outlines the six categories into which the nonvoters divide. That these categories are determined largely by attitudes rather than sociological or economic attributes is one of our most important findings. These new categories of voters and nonvoters also aid those reformers and politicians striving to increase the numbers of voters. To quote Abraham Lincoln: "If we first know who we are and where we are going, we will better know what to do and how to do it."

The second chapter pulls back to look at the long if not particularly glorious history of not voting in America: who was kept from voting and for what reasons, and how those allowed to vote exercised, or failed to exercise, that right.

The third chapter studies each of the six categories of nonvoters in detail both through interviews and analysis of data. The aim is to help you recognize the nonvoters across the road, down the hall, next door, or even behind your own door. The hope is that you will gain new insights about all political behavior including your own, whether you be a voter or a nonvoter. Just as people vote for a variety of reasons, so people refrain from voting for a variety of reasons. Nonvoters are as distinct from each other as are voters. Indeed one of the basic conclusions from our data is that voters and nonvoters are much more alike than was heretofore believed.

The final chapter looks at the various political theories that have dealt with the problem of small voting turnouts: are they harmful or beneficial to democracy? (Philosophers as far apart ideologically as Thomas Jefferson and Karl Marx have been in favor of reduced turnouts.) Next some of the plans being discussed to increase voting turnouts are examined and, unfortunately, many are found wanting. The book concludes with its own proposals, some quite novel, that our data indicate would tend to increase voting turnout.

The technical explanation of how we arrived at our six categories of nonvoters will be found in Appendix A. Much of the data that we obtained will be found in table form in Appendix B. Appropriate citations for the data of others are found in the notes. Teeter intends to pursue other implications of the data over a period of time in various technical journals.

In many ways this book is more of a joint effort than most. Felicity Swayze walked through the door of my press building office with a new master's degree in American Government and Politics. She had the enthusiasm to prowl through masses of reports and statistics and the knowledge to accurately map their terrain; her contribution is reflected on practically every page of this book. Frederick T. Steeper, Vice-President for Political Research of Market Opinion Research, contributed key questions to the survey and helped bring order, insight, and logic out of the initial welter of data. Mary C. Lukens, the Administrator of the Political Research Division, kept perfect track of Teeter's and my papers, comments, and ideas as we went our widely separate ways while researching the data. Karen Lynn Martinsen typed much of the manuscript, interpreting the chicken tracks with speed and skill. And finally there are the nonvoters, to whom thanks must go for being such an interesting, complex, and human group.

Arthur T. Hadley
Washington, D.C.

"For we are a great and special nation in that we regard the man who takes no part in public affairs not as easy going and sensible but as worthless and foul."

Pericles, funeral oration on the dead at Marathon

" 'I tell thee,' said the Grand Inquisitor, 'that man has no greater care and anxiety than to find someone to whom he can hand over this gift of freedom with which he is cursed at birth.' "

The Brothers Karamazov, *Fyodor Dostoyevsky*

"Cherish . . . the spirit of your people and keep alive their attention. . . . If once they become inattentive to public affairs, you and I, and Congress and Assemblies, Judges and Governors, shall all become wolves."

Thomas Jefferson to Edward Carrington

1.

WHO DOES NOT VOTE: MYTH AND FACT

On November 2, 1976, 65 million Americans eligible to vote for President of the United States did not do so—nearly 46 percent of those entitled to enter the voting booth. Who were these people? Why didn't they vote? What reasons and causes kept them from the polls? Ought we to be alarmed, or glad, or indifferent that so many stayed away? And what of our future as those who don't vote approach the political majority?

The election of 1976 had not been dull. Gerald Ford, a popular incumbent, and Jimmy Carter, an attractive newcomer, had campaigned skillfully and hard, right down to the wire, and the contest was decided in a photo finish by a handful of votes. Day after day the all-pervasive campaign continued, featuring bruising primary battles, television debates, and $30 million worth of advertising. Political interest in the South revived; organized labor gave massive support; the polls prophesied a squeaker. The Democratic Party spent $2 million to enroll 3 million new voters. On Election Day perfect voting weather graced the nation coast to coast. Did a high voter turnout result? No. Nonvoting rose again. Close to half the nation's eligible voters avoided the polling booth.

The number of nonvoters in 1976 increased by a full

percentage point over the miserable showing of 1972, when nearly 45 percent of the electorate, or 61 million Americans, shunned the polls. And in 1972 nonvoting had already risen five percentage points above the showing of 1968, when nearly 40 percent of eligible voters stayed home. In short, despite the politicizing influence of Vietnam and Watergate, and despite one of the closest, most intensively reported campaigns in our history, there were more people who didn't vote. Back in 1940, at the end of the Depression, with many recent immigrants still unaccustomed to voting, when only 14 percent of America had a high school education, when there were poll taxes, literacy tests, rigid, often illegal, residency requirements, only 41 percent of eligible voters stayed away. Nonvoting is on the rise. Will the climb continue? Was Carter's victory the important story on that November 3? Or should the record nonvote, again approaching the poor showing of the 1920's, have led the news?

The effect this great mass of nonvoting people will have on our democracy depends on who they are and on why they don't vote. But there have been few nationwide studies designed systematically to compare voters and nonvoters.* Old myths and beliefs have replaced fact, an often dangerous, even fatal process. Those who were bled to cure their fevers during the Middle Ages often died. Before the nonvoters suddenly arise, as they have in the past, to alter our government decisively, we need more knowledge of their beliefs, attitudes, status, and politics.

Voters by their nature and by the act of voting have made a commitment to a party, a cause, an idea. They make basic shifts in their allegiances slowly, if at all. Nonvoters, as we shall see, hold no such convictions. They can shift views or form alliances suddenly, dramatically. Because of the present large pool of nonvoters, the future of our country could substantially change in any coming election. Three important times in our history the number of those not voting has climbed over 45 percent: just before the election of Andrew

---

*The New York Times and CBS conducted an excellent joint poll of voters and nonvoters in 1976. While their poll did not directly focus on who did and did not vote, their data often support my own. With pleasure I tip my hat to their sophisticated methodology and data processing technique.

Jackson, just before the election of Franklin D. Roosevelt, and now.

By contrast, both Abraham Lincoln and the tremendously popular General Dwight Eisenhower were elected at times when there was not such a large pool of nonvoters. They could temporarily gain the allegiance of voters of the opposing party and win, but could effect no major change in party strength or switch in ideology. So the Republican Party came out of the Civil War fighting for its political life, and nearly 100 years later it ended two terms of Dwight Eisenhower still decisively in the minority.

But Andrew Jackson and Franklin Roosevelt were politically blessed with enormous pools of nonvoters. When Andrew Jackson was defeated by John Quincy Adams in 1824, 355,000 people voted. Four years later, when Jackson won, 1,155,000 people voted—an increase of 250 percent. Frontier democracy had arrived. By the end of Jackson's two terms the number of those voting had risen from barely 15 percent of the electorate to 78 percent of those who were eligible to vote. So it was with Franklin Roosevelt. Four years before Roosevelt's election, when Al Smith ran against Herbert Hoover, only 51 percent of the electorate entered the booth. Eight years later Roosevelt entered his second term with 57 percent of the eligibles voting. Among those voting for the first time, Roosevelt's margin of victory was 85 percent.

The nonvoters tamp our political system with an explosive mass, waiting for some trigger to change the course of history.

The image of the nonvoter that traditionally springs to mind is that of Boobus Americanus. Based on 1930's social studies and 1960's civil rights battles, Boobus is seen as a young lunkhead, bombed on beer or stoned on pot, a high school dropout, perhaps a motorcycle-revving white or jiving black, living in the rural South or Northern city slum, dirty, poor, alienated, undereducated, alone. Boobus is also viewed as innocent and powerless. Though educationally and economically handicapped, he or she longs to vote for the best candidates, but is kept from the polls by archaic regulations, meager facilities, and outright fraud laced with violence.

There was a time not too far gone by when such a stereotype contained a dose of truth. Now it's almost pure myth. In our own survey only 13 percent of the nonvoters even came close to the Boobus stereotype. This group included people like Jane N., 38 years old, living on the edge of a housing project just outside Cincinnati, surviving on welfare with a sick husband, four young children, and a married son and his wife living with her, all in five rooms. Jane N., who, when reinterviewed by us in June, could not remember the name of either of the 1976 presidential candidates, did not vote because: "I've got teenagers at home and they don't get along too good. And I have to referee. They're fightin' all the time."

Yet even Jane N. does not perfectly fit the stereotype. She has two political heroes, George Wallace and Ted Kennedy. She is over 30. She recalls voting for Wallace in 1968, as did 17 percent of our nonvoters who voted in that election.

So lend us your tolerance, we come to bury Boobus Americanus, then to raise the true nonvoter in his stead. Item: *The nonvoter is believed to live in the rural South and the slums of the Northern city.* The data show nonvoters only slightly more likely to live in the rural areas of America than voters. In 1976, 25 percent of the nonvoters lived in the country and small towns as against 21 percent of the voters. In its report on the 1972 election, the U.S. Bureau of the Census found 21 percent of both voters and nonvoters living in those areas. Finally in the very heartland of affluence, suburbia itself, we found 31 percent of the 1976 nonvoters and 35 percent of the voters! The 1972 Census report found the same four-point spread between voters and nonvoters living in metropolitan areas outside the central cities as we did. Wherever you may live, the nonvoters are your neighbors—down the road, down the hall, or next door. Perhaps they are even sitting at your table.

For the belief that nonvoters live in the South, there is statistical justification. Thirty-six percent of 1976's nonvoters and 28 percent of the voters came from the South. The Census report for 1972 shows 37 percent of nonvoters living in the South and 28 percent of voters. In both the East and West one's chances of being a nonvoter or a voter are about even. But this distribution conceals a far more dramatic fact about not voting: since the successful civil rights battles of the 1960's, nonvoting is rising rapidly in the North but not in the Deep South.

The voting rate in the North has dropped from 73 percent in 1960 to 58 percent in 1976, a dramatic slide of 15 percent. In the same time period in the South as a whole, voting has gone up. Averaging the figures for 16 Southern states, in 1960 the turnout was 47.4 percent and in 1976 (including the District of Columbia) it was 48.5 percent. Back in 1948, turnout in the South was as low as 25 percent. Between 1960 and 1976 in the Deep South there were dramatic *increases* in voting. In Alabama a rise of 16.5 percent; in Mississippi, up 24.5 percent; and in South Carolina, up 11.1 percent. During the same time dramatic *decreases* in voting occurred in New York, down 16.7 percent; in Iowa, down 12.9 percent; and in Oregon, down 9.5 percent. Undoubtedly a small part of the decline in New York came from the migration of nonvoting blacks into the central city, but what of the drop in Iowa and Oregon? To claim that Boobus Americanus has packed his bags and headed for the deep snows is ridiculous. The nonvoter no longer lives where the stereotype places him.

Item: *The nonvoter group is often believed to be predominantly black.* In our study 14 percent of the nonvoters were black, 81 percent white—hardly a vast number of black nonvoters when one recalls that blacks are 11.4 percent of the American population. It is true that blacks are more inclined not to vote than whites. Thirty-one percent of blacks in our total sample of 2,006 had not voted as compared to 22.8 percent of whites. But this hardly justifies the black nonvoter myth. And again recall the rapidly declining vote in such states as Iowa and Oregon.*

Beyond this, how meaningful is it to label citizens black or white in terms of their not voting? Quite a few of the black nonvoters didn't vote, not because they were black, but because of common characteristics they shared with other nonvoters, black and white.

Louella D. is black, 54 years old, and lives in a housing project at the edge of a small Arkansas town. Louella D. has

---

*A corollary of this myth about the black nonvoter is the myth about the black voter, which alleges that it was this group that elected Jimmy Carter. It wasn't. Blacks voted for Jimmy Carter in the same percentages they voted for George McGovern. In 1972, 47.8 percent of blacks in the South reported voting, and in 1976, 45.7 percent. Lower-middle-class whites in the South, among others, elected Jimmy Carter. This is a fact of political life well understood in the White House, though not by many black politicians and much of the press.

been housebound because of illness for the last three years. She "feels bad, real bad" that she missed the 1976 election. It is only the second one she has missed since she became 21. Mrs. Georgia Q., a black 27-year-old nurse in Toledo, Ohio, watched all three TV debates but just didn't make up her mind until it was too late to register. Now she feels bad. "I feel I haven't fulfilled myself as a citizen; and I feel guilty after I didn't vote." Have we learned anything about why people don't vote by labeling, albeit correctly, these two nonvoters as black nonvoters? Blackness and whiteness today have little bearing on whether someone votes.

Item: *The nonvoter is often believed to be young.* That's true at present. Fifty percent of the nonvoters were under 30, while only 25 percent of the voters were under 30. But again this fact conceals an equally important truth about not voting in America right now. Not voting is growing fastest among those 35 to 44 years old, at a rate of 9.5 percent between 1964 and 1976. In the same period, not voting increased only 5.7 percent among those 21 to 24 years old.* And 50 percent of the nonvoters were over thirty, so just being young is hardly a sole cause of not voting.

Item: *Nonvoters, it is widely believed, tend to be more cynical and alienated from life and government than voters.* We found only a very slight difference between voters and nonvoters in the prevalence of feelings of extreme cynicism about government— about 5 percent. Far more striking was the degree of cynicism expressed by both nonvoters and voters. Forty-nine percent of the voters were highly or somewhat cynical, as were 58 percent of the nonvoters. When the cynicism of the 1976 nonvoters is compared with the cynicism shown by voters polled by the University of Michigan in 1973, today's nonvoters turn out markedly less cynical and alienated than 1973's voters. Of course 1973 was a vintage year for cynicism in America, but the

---

*The greatest rise in not voting from 1972 to 1976 was among the 18- to 21-year-olds. But 1972 had been the first election in which this group were given the vote. They had been the target of special voting campaigns that year. Also the draft for the Vietnam War affected them directly. Even if the decline in the 18- to 21-year-old vote is removed from the national statistics, there is still a decline of 2 percent in turnout between 1972 and 1976. This 2 percent decline is important because the argument is sometimes advanced that voting is actually holding constant (or even increasing) overall and that the 18-year-olds who aren't voting are distorting the statistics. That's not true.

1973 comparison dramatizes the point that voters and non-voters are quite similar in their sense of disaffection with their government.

Both voters and nonvoters expressed to us their dissatisfaction with other major aspects of American life. They both often regarded their work as a bore, their union as something that crimps their pay, hassles them with rules, and then joins with management to screw them. They belonged to few clubs, fraternal or veterans organizations, PTA's, or other groups. Their church is a place in which they got married and from which they will be buried. As for government, that's taxes and more rules and distant, self-serving crooks who lie. Most of their leisure time is spent alone or with family or in small groups. Voters and nonvoters know they cannot stop the world but both are trying to tune out major parts. A widely publicized recent study that concluded cynicism was a major cause of nonvoting failed to ask questions of voters as well as nonvoters. The two groups inhabit the same blasted political landscape, come forth with the same bitter answers. Again one has to look elsewhere for reasons why some vote while others do not.

Item: *Nonvoters are believed to be poorer than voters.* This is true, but the difference certainly cannot account either for the rise or the extent of not voting. Economically, we found that voters and nonvoters are far more alike than different. For example, in the lower-middle to middle-income level, $5,000 to $15,000, where 44 percent of the total sample of voters and nonvoters fell, there were only 6 percent more nonvoters than voters. (Forty-three percent of the voters had incomes of this level as compared to 49 percent of the nonvoters.) At the bottom economic rung, under $5,000, where one might have expected practically everyone to be a nonvoter, there was only an 8 percent difference—15 percent of the voters were from this economic group, and 23 percent of the nonvoters. At the extreme upper end of the scale, over $25,000, where practically everyone is believed to vote, 12 percent of the voters fell in this category and 6 percent of the nonvoters. Income is clearly not a very significant factor in explaining why some vote and others don't. A spread of less than 10 percent at all economic levels gives little support to the image of the nonvoter as Boobus Americanus on welfare or as a tenant farmer.

Item: *Nonvoters are believed to have less education than voters.*
This part of the stereotype is true, though it is becoming less so
each year. Thirty-three percent of the nonvoters had less than
high school education, while only 18 percent of the voters had
failed to graduate from high school. On the other end of the
scale, 43 percent of the voters had attended college, but only 24
percent of the nonvoters. Still that left us with 66 percent of the
nonvoters with a high school education or better, the vast
majority.

Even before our survey there was indirect evidence that
this portion of the nonvoter stereotype was no longer as valid as
it once had been. There was the coincidental rise in both
educational levels and nonvoting. An article of social faith until
the late Sixties had been that as educational levels in America
rose, nonvoting would decline. Yet precisely the opposite
happened. In 1952 only 15 percent of Americans had attended
college. Sixty-one percent had not even graduated from high
school. By 1972, 29 percent had some college, and only 38
percent now failed to graduate from high school. Yet instead of
declining, nonvoting rose by 6 percent during precisely this
period. And the greatest rise occurred among the younger
voters, those with the better education.

Furthermore, nonvoting may actually be rising most
rapidly among those who have completed college. The proof of
this is a bit complex and relies a good deal on indirection and
shading. Since 1960, as measured by the University of Michigan, participation in politics has been falling most rapidly
among the college educated. (Participation in politics is defined
as all those activities that require more effort than voting:
stuffing envelopes, making phone calls, attending meetings,
donating money.) Among those with a college education or
better, participation has declined by 19 percent. Among those
with less than a high school education the decline has been only
4 percent. There are, unfortunately, no comparable measurements of *voting* decline among college graduates. However,
voting and participation are usually assumed to decline at least
at the same rate, though many believe voting declines faster.
These facts indicate that the most rapid rise in nonvoting may
be among the best educated.

Item: *A large number of citizens wish to vote but are prevented
from doing so by difficulty of access to voting facilities, archaic regulations,*

fraud, and even the threat of violence. No part of the Boobus Americanus stereotype is believed in more fervently than this, and
none is further from the truth. Only 12 percent of the nonvoters said they were disenfranchised for reasons of legal
complexity or physical difficulties in getting to the polls. Of
these, one third were unable to meet the residency requirements owing to a recent move. A further one third were out of
town either on election day or during the registration period.

Furthermore, the 12 percent of the nonvoters who gave
physical disenfranchisement as their reason for not voting were
slightly better educated and had higher incomes and fewer
feelings of political impotence than most other nonvoters.
Indeed they discussed politics and national affairs as often as
most voters and showed as much political awareness. Far from
being ignorant and belabored, the majority of those who today
find themselves physically disenfranchised are kept from voting because their success leads to mobility and this causes them
problems in meeting residency requirements. The stereotype
isn't merely wrong; it's backwards.

Yet the myth of the ignorant, poverty-stricken, physically disenfranchised nonvoter continues to be strongly held
for powerful political and psychological reasons.

During the Fifties and early Sixties, when many of
today's officials, activists, and citizens concerned about the
right to vote first entered politics, millions were denied the
right to vote by fraud and violence. For such activists the first
great battle of their lives was for the right of all to vote,
particularly in the South. They remember their great work in
those times with justifiable pride, as their fathers recall D-Day
or Tarawa. But like the draw on Easy Red, those battles to vote
in Selma and elsewhere are over; over and won. Hindrances to
the right to vote still exist—too many of them—but they are
now a minor problem. The literacy test is now unconstitu-
tional, as is the poll tax. Federal officials can and do order the
enrollment of blacks in areas where discrimination exists.

The rise of voting in the South chronicles the destruc-
tion of these physical barriers. In President Carter's home state
of Georgia the percentage of those voting rose in the period
1960–1968 from 29 percent to 43 percent; in Mississippi it rose
from 25 percent to 53 percent, in Louisiana from 45 percent to
55 percent. By way of dramatic contrast, over the same period

the turnout in Minnesota—which consistently has one of the best records in the nation—declined from 76 percent to 74 percent. The battle to secure the right to vote in practice as well as in theory has been won. But like most veterans of successful wars, the veterans of the civil rights struggle refight old battles. The stereotype lives on.

Unfortunately, the belief that the nonvoter is mired in ignorance and apathy and fenced in by violence and quasi-legal restraints also continues to exist for less honorable reasons. The stereotype fills a psychic craving for self-justification on both the extreme right and left of American politics. The violent conservative sees the nonvoter as someone basically worthless and easily led who fortunately is kept outside the democratic system and should remain there. In this view, if they ever began to vote, any demagogue could grab their attention and destroy democracy. The radical extremist sees the ignorant but noble nonvoter as kept from the polls by violence and deceit. This belief then supplies further proof of the hypocrisy and evil of America in which he or she so delights.

Finally politicians support the myth, consciously or unconsciously, because it serves their purpose. They would much rather claim that nonvoters wish to vote but are kept outside the system for lack of needed "reforms," than face the unpleasant fact that voters voluntarily avoid the booth in droves because of their contempt for politicians and also because they see no connection between politics and their lives.

The election returns themselves are unequivocal on this point. Between 1960 and 1976 the increase in nonvoting nationally was about 9 percent. Leading this upward surge of nonvoting were precisely those states where by common consent voting and registration are easiest. North Dakota, where even registration is unnecessary, is generally conceded to be the easiest state in which to vote. In the 1960–1976 period nonvoting rose by 9.1 percent in North Dakota. Registration by mail is generally conceded to be the next easiest form of registration. Yet in ten of the eighteen states that had some form of mail registration, the rise in nonvoting between 1960 and 1976 was greater than the national average. Such easy-to-vote-in states as New York had a 16.7 percent rise in nonvoting over the period (about 7 percent over the national average); Iowa had a 12.9 percent rise; California, 14.4 percent; New Jersey, 12.3 percent; Delaware, 13.7 percent; Pennsylvania, 15.6 percent. A recent study also notes that between 1972 and 1976 "combined turnout in all states with mail registration declined about 2 percentage points, but turnout showed no decline in states without mail registration." Ease of access to the booth and the numbers of those voting no longer correlate.

Yet politicians and others continue to write, talk, and act as if there were a great mass of potential voters out there being kept from the polls by legal tricks and fraud. For example, after the 1976 election Alexander E. Barkan, a knowledgeable old-timer who heads COPE, the AFL/CIO political action arm, writing on "The Myth of Voter Apathy," claimed: "Millions more would have turned out [to vote in 1976] had they been able simply to get in line election day and make their choice known. . . . In Wisconsin, a recently enacted state law permits voters to forget about registration entirely, just walk up on election day, provide a driver's license or other proof of age and residence and go into the booth and pull the levers. About 200,000 unregistered Wisconsinites voted November 2, creating an actual increase in voting percentage over 1972."

But these numbers have been carefully selected for a political purpose; they conceal, not enlighten. It is true that in 1976 the turnout in Wisconsin was greater than in 1972, the year of Nixon versus McGovern. But the 1976 Wisconsin turnout was actually down a full percentage point from 1968, when voters still had to register 30 days before an election.*

Yet politicians continually point to Wisconsin and Minnesota, where turnouts are high and legal restrictions on voting few, to prove that in other parts of the nation voters are physically disenfranchised. They never mention that the proportion of those voting has declined in those two states in recent years, or explain that their commendably high turnouts stem from their political and cultural heritage.

Let us try to explode this most persistent part of the nonvoter stereotype with one final small burst of fact. Minnesota is the state with the best turnout in the nation—71.6

---

*The enfranchisement of the 18- to 20-year-olds in 1972 complicates but does not change the thrust of these statistics.

percent in 1976—and also with easy access to the booth. Yet between 1960 and 1970 the vote in Minnesota declined 4.8 percent—and in 1976 a Minnesotan was even on the ballot as vice-presidential candidate for the Democratic Party! Non-voting is on the rise everywhere. Voters are no longer significantly held back from the booth.

In many other areas in which voters and nonvoters are traditionally thought to be different we found them similar. There were no significant differences between voters and nonvoters in religion, in sex, or in ethnic background. Nor did the voters and nonvoters vary much in how they saw the presidential race. Eighty-five percent of the nonvoters felt the election would be very close or somewhat close, while 90 percent of the voters felt the same way, hardly a difference that would account for the fact that close to half the country did not vote. Indeed, 63 percent of all nonvoters correctly saw the election as being *very* close and still didn't vote. Nor in many aspects of their personal lives were the voters and nonvoters all that different. They shared the same worries, joys, fears, and problems.

In these findings of similarity we are supported by Bernard J. Bookbinder, an editor of the Long Island, New York, paper *Newsday*, whose political and sociological studies of Nassau and Suffolk counties on Long Island are masterpieces of information. In his two counties Bookbinder found no difference between voter and nonvoter in religion, sex, or ethnic background, nor did he find any difference between voters and nonvoters as to whether they were liberals, moderates, or conservatives. We found roughly the same pattern nationally, though we did find the nonvoters less likely to know into which ideological category they fell.

This question of whether most of the nonvoters are liberal or conservative has caused a great many commentators difficulty. Scores of politicians have gone haring off either after some conservative "silent majority" or some radical "new majority." The truth is that the nonvoters are in the main neither strongly liberal nor strongly conservative. Rather they are people without strong political commitments. They like to believe they were with the winner. During the Eisenhower years when nonvoters were asked after Ike's 1956 victory how they would have voted, they were for Ike better than 2 to 1. After

Kennedy's victory they were Democratic, 1.5 to 1. After Lyndon Johnson's landslide they were Democratic by 2 to 1. With Nixon's victory they shifted back to become Republicans after the fact by 2 to 1. After they know you are a winner the nonvoters are with you all the way. Again they aren't so different from the rest of us.

The more that nonvoter and voter were measured in traditional ways, the more surprisingly alike they looked. Old beliefs plainly did not account for the present dramatic rise in not voting.

Turnout figures also mask the liars, those who report to innocent pollsters that they do vote when in fact they do not. The U.S. Bureau of the Census, showing the predictable desire of the bureaucracy not to offend those who help pay its bills, euphemistically labels these liars "overreporters." These citizens represent a difficult problem for all researchers, one that while expensive and time-consuming to study, needs far closer examination than we, unfortunately, have been able to afford.

The pioneering work on this phenomenon has been done by political scientist Aage Clausen. Using his own delicate labeling, he calls overreporting "response error." He refers to overreporters as those who indulge in what they perceive to be "a harmless little fiction." He finds their number, in the estimates of turnout produced by the Census Bureau, as not less than 3 percent and not more than 8 percent. Clausen, however, makes few attempts to identify who the overreporters are.

The Census Bureau itself now finds the number of overreporters fluctuating between 5 and 7 percent from election to election. We began polling the night of the election because experience shows that people will more likely tell you the truth immediately after an event, later remembering a more idealized version of their actions. Still we know overreporters could be at least 10 percent of our voters. When we went back in May and June to do detailed follow-up interviews with some 100 of the 2,006 we had polled, we found a few who now told us they had voted but who earlier had said they had not. Interestingly enough, they now all claimed to have voted for Carter.

The problem then becomes one of trying to figure who the liars are. In what ways are they distorting the picture of both voter and nonvoter?

While working on this book, acquaintances would tell me what a great idea it was, since voting was so important. Often they would then be reminded by spouses, friends, or even children that they themselves had not voted in the last election. The Census Bureau, which runs a sophisticated and detailed, if cautious, operation, says that so far they haven't been able to come up with any conclusions on their over-reporters, that all they have is "a bunch of numbers." Teeter, polling in 1972, discovered that the group most likely to say they had voted when they hadn't were upper-middle-income Democrats. Here again Bookbinder at *Newsday* has done some interesting work.

Bookbinder discovered, by checking the actual registration records on Long Island against the responses of those who claimed to be registered, that 26 percent of those who asserted that they were registered to vote in fact were not. Moreover, and this is the fascinating nub, he found that while 54 percent of those who had *not* graduated from high school said they were registered when they were not, fully 78 percent of those who *had* graduated from college said they were registered when they were not. Unfortunately, with our nationwide sample and finite resources, we were unable to check on where our overreporting occurred. But our definite feeling from the data is that Bookbinder is again correct. Specifically our survey discloses a number of higher-income, better-educated, white male voters who have all the peculiar characteristics (which will be described later) of our nonvoters. A portion of these almost certainly did not vote.

To quote Bookbinder: "High income college graduates were in fact far more likely than others to state they were registered, when in fact they weren't." When survey data are adjusted by sophisticated means to offset the effect of the liars, the supposed traditional differences between voters and nonvoters become even hazier—where they do not vanish altogether.

With the traditional view of the nonvoter now buried, let us proceed to examine who the nonvoters are. But one problem remains. The very term "nonvoter" is misleading. Not only does it carry overtones of the stereotype, by popular usage it also has come to imply a negative judgment. Nonvoters are commonly thought to lack something. The term is derogatory.

Such negative baggage blocks understanding of why Americans don't vote. As a result throughout the rest of the book the noun "nonvoter" will be used sparingly. In preference, those who do not vote will be called "refrainers." Refraining makes no moral judgments. Some people vote. Others refrain. Refrainers can be able people, know a great deal about politics, about the world. Many lead full lives. But they have taken, sometimes consciously, sometimes unconsciously, a decision to refrain from voting.

Paul G. is typical of a whole class of refrainers, about 35 percent of the sample. He is 37 years old, is making good money as a route salesman for a soft drink company, and is married with two children, one twelve years old, the other two and a half. His wife brings in additional income as a linguistics teacher at a local school. They live in a pleasant ranch-style house in suburban New Jersey with the beach almost in the backyard. Once a week Paul commutes to New York City, where he is working toward his master's degree in psychology. It seems to Paul that life is just too full, too good for him to be interested in politics. He feels that politicians generally do a good job. "Maybe, though, when I finish this [Master's program]," he says, "I will get interested. . . . Right now political affiliations are just not part of my planning."

Gloria E., who works in the city manager's office of a western Florida city, detailed the abuses she had seen around city hall that turned her into a refrainer. "When politicians are not interested in you, you lose interest in them," she said. "Who cares for us?"

George U. is 26 years old and having problems because he hasn't graduated from high school. We interviewed him at his mother's home in St. Louis, where he was studying for his equivalency examination. He doesn't care enough about politicians or politics to vote, and he believes former President Ford "loused things up. . .didn't work things too well." However, he was able to discuss in some detail Carter's plan for a tax on big cars and gasoline and its effect on poor people like himself, who bought the big cars third or fourth hand "and are just a poor slob putting gas in. They can't afford to pay a tax or replace the car."

Backing up such interviews of our own, Haynes Johnson, a senior writer for *The Washington Post* who raises sociological reporting to a fine art, wrote from Point Reyes, California, just before the 1976 election: "What's different this time is more than the numbers of people who say they won't vote. It's who they are and what they represent. . . . They tend to be among the better educated and better informed."

There is a secondary benefit from the use of the term "refrainer." Not only does it make it easier to understand who the "nonvoters" are, it also helps keep the striking similarities between voters and refrainers in mind. This is important because present efforts to increase turnout focus almost exclusively on the refrainer, so a key question is forgotten: how to keep voters voting? The increase in not voting doesn't just come from refrainers continuing to refrain. It stems in part from voters becoming refrainers. Twenty-one percent of the sample of voters had characteristics that made them more like refrainers than many of the refrainers themselves. Of course, many of the overreporters are located in this group, but many others in this category are certainly still held as voters by the slenderest of threads. They need help too. It's fine to bring the prodigal son home, but those laboring in the heat of the day, voting for years, need help too. Some are about to desert the booth unless we do something. The use of the term "refrainer" helps us remember the many, many voters on the verge of refraining.

 So we find that voters are separated from refrainers not, as previously thought, by barriers of class, economics, location, and education, but primarily by their view of life. To use the language of political science, the differences between voters and refrainers are attitudinal rather than socioeconomic. Nor do we find physical and legal restraints to be any longer a major cause of not voting. There are still a few inequities, but these, as we shall see, surprisingly operate against the middle class rather than against the traditional "nonvoter."

The discovery that attitudes, not simply sociological attributes, make the refrainer runs like an Ariadne thread through the twists and turning of our findings. Further, these attitudes do not correlate, as would be supposed, with attributes such as sex, race, wealth. Rather they group in their own way to form the basic reasons why some people vote and others do not; a fact that helps explain why voters and refrainers often appear similar. Finally, clusters of these attitudes can help us distinguish among the types of refrainers and aid in predicting which groups of refrainers are most likely to enter, or reenter, the booth. This knowledge, in turn, makes more understandable the effect on our politics if and when the refrainers start to vote.

The close examination of all refrainers falls into two equally important parts. First there are several general attitudes about life and politics that most refrainers hold and most voters do not. There are also some other attitudes that voters and refrainers hold in common which indicate future trends in refraining. Second there are different reasons for refraining that divide the refrainers from each other. Those who don't vote are often regarded as a monolithic entity. They're not. Though they usually hold certain broad beliefs in common, beneath these they divide into six very different groups of people.

To take up the general attitudes that separate voters from refrainers first, one of the most important of our discoveries we truly stumbled upon. As we set out to explore the terra incognita of the refrainers, we were like Lewis and Clark trying to cross the nation. There were charts of the edges of the country and some reports from the interior, but how should we go? Frederick Steeper, a Teeter associate and an admirer of Professor Edward Banfield's distinctions between people who planned and those who trusted to luck, suggested that we place a plan/luck question on the survey. Somewhat hesitantly we did. We wanted to keep the survey short and everyone had ten favorite questions he or she wanted asked. And lo, the stone that the builders almost rejected yielded extraordinary results.

Voters and refrainers divided from each other over whether life was largely a matter of planning or of luck as they did over nothing else. Of the voters, 57 percent believed life was a matter of planning, only 38 percent found life more a matter of luck. For the refrainers these statistics dramatically reversed. Fifty-four percent of the refrainers believed life to be largely a matter of luck, and only 37 percent believed in planning ahead. Such wide, strong relationships on questions of attitude are highly unusual. These results indicated that the traditional image of the "nonvoter" would have to be drastically altered.*

Sex affected little whether people believed in plan or luck. Fifty-two percent of the male refrainers believed life more a matter of luck, as did 57 percent of the females. We expected a vast difference between old and young, since the old are more likely to be involved in the intricate web of an ordered life. That difference was not there; the percentage of planners and luckers held constant across age groups. Equally surprising was the fact that the percentage of refrainers who believed in planning as against those who believed in luck held almost constant as incomes rose. Indeed, at the very highest income level of the sample, $25,000 and over, where one would have expected practically everyone to be a planner, no more refrainers believed in planning than in luck.

Frank D. is 21 years old, takes pride in his skill as a plastic extrusion press operator and is hopeful that Ted Kennedy will some day run for president. Much as he liked his job he felt that getting it, or rising to be a supervisor "was luck, mostly bad luck [said with a laugh], but luck." Mary P., three years older, lives with her husband and two children two miles from the center of a small Utah town. She failed to vote because of the complications of moving and the distance to the polling place. She too stresses luck. "A lot of things in life are a matter of luck. . . . The people around me that are really able to get ahead, they came into money from their parents. Their parents gave them things." Mrs. Bea H., 29, lives in central Pennsylvania, where her husband is a maintenance man for the university. He doesn't vote either. She looks forward to moving to the country. "If we ever do get our own land we'll put up a trailer or something." For her it's luck too. Last year, just as they got nearly all their bills paid, their boy had an unexpected operation, "You never know what will come up."

The more affluent refrainers say the same things about life and luck. Mrs. Muriel T., 29 years old, with four children, has a husband who is a railroad engineer, a good middle-class job, and they own their own home on the outskirts of a railroad town in central Kansas. "I don't plan ahead on anything, I go

---

*We asked the question "Do you think it's better to plan your life way ahead, or would you say life is too much a matter of luck to plan ahead very far?" The possible answers were (1) plan ahead, (2) too much a matter of luck, or (3) don't know.

day to day." That goes for the family books, which they keep together. "But just to pay for what comes up." Edward E., a black truck driver who puts in long hours hauling vegetables between Nogales and Los Angeles, is 49 years old. He makes just under $15,000 a year and is pretty happy with his job and life. "When you drive a truck you know life's a lot of luck."

Two older women, both over 50 and half the country apart, used practically the same words in describing luck, voting, and life, though one had only graduated from grade school and was unhappy, while the other was a college graduate enjoying life. Sally F.'s husband used to work for the Air Force and they just retired to a farm on the Alabama-Mississippi border. She said: "I don't think my vote makes a lot of difference. Things keep turning out." Paula D., in the suburbs outside of Indianapolis said: "I don't feel my vote makes much difference. I feel it's going to go the way it's supposed to regardless of what I do."

So it goes, cleaving through age, sex, and economic background, an almost Oriental feeling among most refrainers that one rides a wheel of chance.

There were, of course, the more than a third of the refrainers who believed in planning ahead. This group, frankly, tended to look a bit more like voters than like the rest of their fellow refrainers. For example, they were more likely to have voted at least once than were other refrainers. Forty-five percent of the refrainers who were planners said they had voted in the 1972 election—the next to most recent election and therefore the one most likely to be remembered accurately—whereas only 29 percent of those who believed in luck said they had done so. Also our refrainers who believed in planning were happier, were a bit less likely to think the people running the government were all crooks, and were better educated.*

The plan/luck response and other constellations of attitudes were used to help us assign to refrainers their basic reason for not voting. As an extreme example, suppose a 55-year-old woman cited reasons of health for not going to the polls. If she believed in planning, had voted many times before,

*These refraining planners were also more likely to be male than female, 56 percent men compared to 44 percent women. We will go into why in some detail later, because this little statistic when analyzed reveals an interesting social truth.

was happy, had feelings of political power, and was only mildly cynical, one could be almost certain that bad health had kept her from the polls. If another 55-year-old woman citing health believed in luck, had never voted, had extreme feelings of political impotence, was extremely cynical and unhappy, she would fall into another category. Not all decisions were as easy as these examples. Refrainers are human beings and as such show pleasantly human resistance against being typed.

Note how far away from the nonvoter stereotype we are in defining voters and refrainers by their belief in planning against luck. We are talking about a basic attitude of people toward life no matter what their income, education, or age. Has a belief in chance been growing recently among Americans? Are we coming more and more to doubt our abilities to control our destiny? Unfortunately, there are no analyzed data available over a long period of time to provide answers. But the growth in not voting would indicate that more and more Americans feel their lives are spinning out of control.

Another fascinating difference between voters and refrainers lay in the feelings of political impotence expressed by refrainers. Here there is a complex problem. If you measure the feelings of *extreme* powerlessness, you find only a 9 percent difference between voters and refrainers. This is because there is a group of voters, 21 percent of the voter sample, who are very much like refrainers and about whom we will have more to say later. Members of this group are quite likely to stop voting at any moment. These particular voters feel the same degree of extreme political impotence as many of the refrainers, so they distort comparisons of voter to refrainer, making them seem more alike than they are. Once this group is removed, the details become clear. Most voters feel politically efficacious. Most refrainers feel politically impotent. Feelings of political impotence play a definite part in refraining.

The three questions on political efficacy, which are used to measure feelings of political impotence, are, first: "People like me don't have any say about what the government does." Less than one half of the refrainers, 43 percent, expressed feelings of political power by disagreeing with this statement. However, better than one-half, 59 percent of the voters, disagreed, a difference of 16 percent. Question two was: "Sometimes politics and government seem so complicated that a person like me can't really understand what's going on." A

majority of both voters and refrainers agreed with this statement, but there was a 10 percent difference between the two
groups: 72 percent of the refrainers agreed with the statement
as against 62 percent of the voters. The final question was: "I
don't think public officials care much what people like me
think." This produced the biggest spread between refrainers
and voters, 17 percent. While 52 percent of the voters felt
public officials cared about them, only 35 percent of the
refrainers felt so.* Fifty-five percent of refrainers felt public
officials did not care, and 10 percent didn't know. When
the politically impotent voters were removed, the difference
between voters and refrainers rose dramatically on this question to 31 percent. To be classed as extreme political im-
potents, voters or refrainers had to agree with all three of these
questions.

    Feelings of political impotence are not the same as
feelings of political cynicism, though they are often confused.
Feelings of political impotence rest on the belief you can't
control things in government. Feelings of political cynicism rest
on the belief that those running the government are a bunch of
lying crooks, trying to separate you from your last nickle. Voter
and refrainer rather surprisingly agree almost completely that
you can seldom trust the government. Thus cynicism is not a
 significant factor in the decision to refrain.

    Forty-nine percent of the voters studied were at the high
end of the cynicism scale, as were 58 percent of refrainers, a
moderate difference of 9 percent. Nor were these percentages
greatly changed when we began removing various categories of
voters and refrainers and comparing those who were left. Here
the University of Michigan's Survey Research Center figures, as
well as others, support our findings. Their measurements find
the same degree of cynicism among their voters as we find
among both our voters and refrainers....** Sixty-seven percent

---

*Alert readers familiar with voting behavior will note that 1976's refrainers agreed with
this statement that public officials don't care in almost the exact percentages as the
University of Michigan's voters in 1973, 55 percent and 56 percent respectively. It is
also interesting to note that the data show less impotence on this question among voters
than in the 1973 Michigan group, but nonvoting is rising—proving once again the
complexity of the vote-refrain decision.

**This would seem an appropriate place for another heartfelt expression of thanks, this
time to Norman H. Nie, Sidney Verba, and John R. Petrocik for their skillful blending of
political theory and statistics in *The Changing American Voter*.

of the Michigan survey voters in 1973 and 64 percent of the refrainers in our survey felt that government is run for the benefit of a few. Also in 1973, 66 percent of the University of Michigan's respondents felt you could trust government to do what is right only some of the time. Fifty-one percent of the voters and 56 percent of the refrainers in our survey felt the same way. In 1973, voters were highly cynical. The 1973 data do not include nonvoters but it is unlikely they would be less cynical. Voter and refrainer swim in the same polluted political sea, and the tide of cynicism has been rising carrying them both forward. The 21 percent of our voters who were extremely impotent were also much more cynical than the refrainers.

Several other recent studies that measured cynicism, particularly *The New York Times*–CBS poll and Bernard Bookbinder's research, have found little difference between voter and refrainer. *New York Times*–CBS found merely one percentage point separating voters and refrainers on two questions of political cynicism. Bookbinder concluded; "People who don't register are no more likely to be cynical about politics or politicians than people who register."*

Though the level of cynicism among voters and refrainers does not differ greatly, the degree and fury of it expressed during our in-depth interviews is staggering.

"I'm not foolin' with either side anymore. In the beginning we were a Christian people, or we claimed to be; and Christian people should not fool with what politics has come to be." So spoke Mims T., a retired construction worker living on his social security payments in rural Virginia. Emma E. was born on a farm in Missouri and wishes for another Harry Truman. She and her husband had to move from their home of 23 years in Erie, Pennsylvania, because the neighborhood became too rough. "They got more crooks in Pennsylvania than in the whole U.S." says Emma E. "If they're not a crook when they get in they're crooked afterwards." She and her husband don't see themselves ever voting again. "Not unless you get a man in there you can believe. How would you know?" Elizabeth U., a secretary in Humble, Texas, a town right on the outskirts of Houston, states: "I believe the system will be changed by God's will. To get involved now is wrong."

---

*A small caveat here. There is some indication that as education increases extreme cynicism may become important as a reason for not voting.

Gloria E., the city government worker in western Florida who sees politics from the inside, says: "Things are not done with people in mind. They [the politicians] promise you everything and then you get nothing. Look at Watergate. What else can I say. Labor unions and big corporations they do the same thing. One hand wipes the other. The big boys rule." Alonzo W., well off as a school administrator in central Texas, states sadly that "Nixon was not at all the type of individual I thought I had voted for." This has affected his whole attitude toward politics. In York, Pennsylvania, Pease D., still working as a security guard at 70, voices the same thoughts. "I just sort of lost confidence, especially since that Watergate. That almost tore the country apart as much as Vietnam." In Indianapolis young James W. saw his Democratic mother being forced to swear she was a Republican before she could get a county job, and he decided to refrain. Carlo N. of Brownsville, Texas, whose family is giving him the summer in Europe as a high school graduation present, says: "I'd be more likely to vote if a candidate were honest."

Again the similarity between voters and refrainers should be stressed. There are a great many voters who feel the truth of the statements just quoted. Unless politics in America changes, many of these voters may become refrainers. Haynes Johnson of *The Washington Post*, discussing the reasons why voters become refrainers, uses the word "betrayal." Many refrainers, he feels, have voted once or worked for a particular candidate and, in this America of instant gratification, when that candidate lost or turned out to be less than the man they had hoped, these people ceased voting. It didn't matter whether that candidate was Barry Goldwater, or Eugene McCarthy, or George Wallace, or George McGovern, or Richard Nixon. The fact of the defeat or the betrayal led to the same result: refraining.

The deep cynicism expressed by voters and nonvoters may often be accounted for in the following way. Politics has become disconnected from the lives of many people. Since they don't see what politicians and politics are doing for them, they become suspicious and resentful. Twenty years ago getting a raise, getting promoted, starting one's own business, in addition to being important life goals, were seen as connected with politics. People believed that whether the Republicans or Democrats were in office effected their chances of getting ahead. Now the importance of these goals has faded and other questions become more important: recreation, education, a home in the country. People don't see any link between those present goals and politics. So they come to look on politicians as people who spend their tax money, without producing.

One final, brief generalization about refrainers, but an important one. Practically every one of those we reinterviewed believed voting to be a moral obligation. They felt it their responsibility to vote and most of them felt bad that they hadn't. Almost all of them remembered their parents voting, or thought they did—some even their grandparents. They re- called specific incidents about their parents on election day which indicated the almost mystic appeal of voting, an attitude that was reflected in part in a 1956 University of Michigan survey. The survey found that less than 6 percent of their respondents had a sense of "citizen duty" that was so low that it could possibly lead to not voting. For the refrainers in 1976 the feeling of moral obligation to vote was so strong that it would probably be impossible to set up a panel of refrainers and study their shifts in attitudes over a period of time. Participation in such a panel would turn most of its members from refrainers to voters.

Bookbinder of *Newsday* found that 94 percent of his interviewees felt voting was a moral obligation. In our study, the percentage of refrainers who felt this way was the same. Though as we shall see, there was a group of refrainers, 6 percent, who seemed to feel just the opposite. Definitely however, the act of refraining has not led the vast majority of refrainers to despise the vote. Far from it. They still have a flag-waving faith in the booth. They might avoid entering its doors, but they would fight any wrecking crew that openly tried to tear it down.

So much for the general attitudes that, though some- times showing voters and refrainers to be surprisingly similar, usually separate them from each other. Equally important, our data enabled us to divide refrainers among themselves ac- cording to the dominant reason for their not voting. Most previous studies of voting behavior focused on sociological differences between voters and nonvoters. They looked for statistical correlations between such factors as income, sex, religion, race, age, and voting. This approach had two unfor- seen results. First, it tended to overlook the striking similarities between voters and refrainers, such as their mutual cynicism. Second, the search for correlations and linkages, focusing on universal behavior, failed to notice the marked differences among types of refrainers. It is true to say that nonvoters are, on the whole, poorer than voters but such a statement deflects attention from those 28 percent of all refrainers who make over $15,000 a year.

For example, to point out that a highly educated, middle-aged, upper-income, deeply religious suburban businessman is more likely to vote than a low-income, rural, Southern, high school dropout, under 21, is entirely true but hardly a jaw-dropping observation. And it doesn't help explain why refraining is rising rapidly among educated suburbanites and decreasing slightly among poor Southerners. It's like saying that slum-dwelling, undernourished sweatshop workers are more likely to have tuberculosis than college-educated football players. That's no surprise either and doesn't explain much about the tubercle bacillus.

Our data revealed that refrainers divide into six major categories. Some of these groupings involve brand new ways of looking at refraining. I must stress that this is almost the first voyage through this territory. Like Lewis and Clark mapping America, I know there is more out there. Others will fill in gaps in these maps, the sooner the better. The marked differences among refrainers, besides being fascinating in themselves, tell us a great deal about today's America. Understanding these differences enables those who wish to attack the problem of not voting to see where they are going.

To develop the six groups we began with the reasons the refrainers volunteered for their not voting. The initial categories bore such headings as "not interested," "too busy," "sick," "just didn't," "couldn't decide," "didn't like the candidates." Then, as we combined some new insights with elements of the conventional wisdom, made new data runs, pored through the questionnaires and reinterviews, new and original patterns emerged. These finally distilled into the book's six categories of refrainers. To my surprise, I found defining the categories among the most fascinating work I have ever done.

The refrainers divided as follows:

1. *The Positive Apathetics* (35 percent of the refrainers). These are people who refrain from voting because their lives

are going so well that voting seems irrelevant. They are educated, happy, well-off—the very group that heretofore experts
believed voted. But these people are apathetic not out of misery
and dissatisfaction, rather out of contentment. The number of
positive apathetics is probably greater than 35 percent, because
these refrainers have the characteristics of the overreporters,
those who don't vote yet say they do. These refrainers are about
as far removed from the stereotyped nonvoter as possible.
Though they are more likely to believe in luck than the voters,
they are less likely to believe in luck than the other groups of
refrainers.

2. *The Bypassed* (13 percent of the refrainers). These
refrainers are most like the traditional "nonvoter." They have
low incomes and little education. Many of them have never
voted or have voted once, often for George Wallace. They have
a hard time following political campaigns and in our detailed
interviews were uninformed in the majority of their answers.
They don't just drop out of politics; they have been bypassed by
most of America, affluence, education, choice, even often the
joys of family life. Most of the governmental programs to
increase voting are aimed at these bypassed refrainers, as-
suming them to represent the vast majority of nonvoters. The
data show that not only is this group of refrainers relatively
small, but it contains people who are not likely to vote under
almost any circumstances. They are our hard-core refrainers.

3. *The Politically Impotent* (22 percent of the refrainers).
These are the refrainers who feel that nothing they can say or
do, including vote, affects their government. They feel they
have no control over their political, and often their private,
lives. These refrainers are sometimes referred to as "alienated."
"Politically impotent" seems a more accurate, though not as
glamorous a term, because many of these people aren't hostile
toward politics and they often remain attached to their community, church, or family. In fact they are doing as well in
society as many other people. It's a precise feeling of helpless-
ness over politics that leads to their refraining, the "*Ich bin nur
ein kleiner Mann*" syndrome.

4. *The Physically Disenfranchised* (18 percent of the refrainers). These are the people who for legal or physical
reasons, including bad health, are unable to vote. The most
commonly cited physical reason was bad health, 6 percent of all

our refrainers. The most commonly cited legal reason was the inability to meet residency requirements after a recent move. Complex registration procedures and hard-to-find voting places, the traditionally conceived causes of refraining, were cited by only 2 percent of the refrainers. For this group particular care was used to refine the data, in order to make certain physical disenfranchisement was the true reason and not merely an excuse given out of shame for not voting.

5. *The Naysayers* (6 percent of the refrainers). These are the people whose pride it is not to vote. They know why they refrain and are willing to tell you, often at greater length than you care to hear. They have a great deal of information about politics but have decided that voting is somehow wrong. For them refraining is a highly conscious choice, often almost an act of defiance.

6. *The Cross-Pressured* (5 percent of the refrainers). The interesting thing here is that there are so few of them. While this group is definitely not part of the usual nonvoter stereotype, sophisticated social scientists, politicians, and reporters, including this one, have long believed quite a few cross-pressured nonvoters existed. Though other criteria than our own could turn up a few more people, cross-pressured refrainers would still remain but a small percentage. These refrainers have a lot of information about politics, they want to vote, but they just can't make up their minds between the two candidates. They might be the children of Democratic parents who don't like the Democratic ballot choices but still don't want to vote Republican. Or an Italian-American boy from Rochester, New York, where Italian-Americans are Democratic, marries an Italian-American girl from Cambridge, Massachusetts, where Italian-Americans are Republican. Result: refraining. In the past, when local ties, family ties, and party loyalty were stronger, there undoubtedly were more such cross-pressured nonvoters, but today such cords bind loosely, if at all. In close campaigns some politicians deliberately try to force the other candidates' potential voters into this category—for example, increase the worries of Northern liberal Democrats about Carter's southern Baptist religion, or play on the fears of conservative Republicans about Ford's reliance on Henry Kissinger.

Naturally not all refrainers fit neatly into one category or another. To put some here and others there is, in the jargon of today, "judgmental." There are naysayers with extreme feelings of political impotence, bypassed refrainers who yet believe in planning and may be truly physically disenfranchised, cross-pressured refrainers who report agony in making up their minds but who are happy, educated, and wealthy and may be positive apathetics.

For example, Ben O. is a happy-go-lucky 23-year-old who makes a nice living as a supervisor in a motorcycle repair shop outside of Sacramento, California, and lives with his parents while he searches for his own apartment. Ben felt that "No matter who I vote for, I don't think it will make any difference to me at all. It's a lesser of two evils sort of thing. . . . I think the biggest worry is how one man dresses and another combs his hair. . . . They [politicians] don't have anything to do with me." Since Ben, a college graduate, is making a good living, particularly for his age, and has other attributes of a positive apathetic, we placed him in that category. But he is also quite adamant that there is little to choose from between politicians, which gives him some of the attributes of a naysayer.

Jean K. is in her mid-thirties and lives in rural Nebraska, where her husband works for the power company. Her answers to our three political efficacy questions indicate extreme political impotence. She believes: "I don't know enough about politics to vote." She is placed in the politically impotent category. But Jean K. has some college, is happy with her life, likes where she lives, and is reasonably well off. These are all marks of the positive apathetic. People, being complex, resist being forced into even the most accurate of categories.

The problem is particularly acute with those who gave as their reason for refraining that they were out of town on election day, had recently moved, didn't have transportation, and other such physical reasons. Unless they were "very much interested" in who won the election and indicated that they had followed politics by being able to identify the candidates and some other political figures, the people giving such answers were placed in other categories than physically disenfranchised. On the other hand, those who cited reasons of ill health for not voting were left in the ill-health category if they were either "very" or "somewhat interested" in who won the election and if they knew something about politics. Our feeling was that those in ill health could well have had other fears and interests on their minds.

These are rapid sketches of the refrainers. The book now turns aside from interviews and data for a chapter to look at the history of political refraining in the United States. Americans have a tendency to treat all problems as if they were born yesterday. Not voting is no such new-hatched chick. It has a long, fascinating, if not particularly distinguished, history in our land.

2.

REFRAINING: FROM PLYMOUTH ROCK THROUGH THE NEW DEAL

The political baggage carried ashore by the first settlers in the new world bore labels reading "Made in Britain." In England, since the mythic meeting at Runnymede in 1215 that produced the Magna Carta, an ever-widening circle of people had been able to wrest from the King some control over their destinies. First the great nobles acquired political rights, then the lesser nobles, then all the landed gentry. In fact, by the 1400's, the voting/nonvoting cycle was in one of its periodic swings and Parliament, believing that the franchise had been extended too widely, had moved to restrict the vote.

Parliament noted that "a very great and excessive number of people" had been voting, each of them claiming "a voice equivalent with the most worthy knights and squires." The British government then proceeded to limit the right to vote to "forty-shilling freeholder," owners of property from which a rent of 40 shillings or more per year was derived. This property represented a substantial investment and the yeomen so enfranchised were often richer than the lord. However, the political fact of life was that Parliament had acted to increase the number of refrainers.

This action illustrates the twin themes that will continually lace through this brief history of American refraining:

the first, *who is allowed to vote?* and the second, *who among those so allowed fail to exercise their rights and why?* For example, from the period of the first settling of America until 1920 women were legally excluded from the vote, as are the insane, the felon, and those under eighteen now. Before 1920, the reason women did not vote was, clearly, always political; afterwards, it was only sometimes political, but more often social or psychological. At times political and social restraints merge. A group may be technically able to vote, but the physical restraints may be so great, as were those on blacks in the South until the mid-Sixties, that only the most highly motivated go to the polls. Today many high school and college refrainers, embarrassed about not voting, will, when first questioned, claim physical disenfranchisement. But under more detailed probing, their reasons turn out to be psychological and social.

The first colonists to arrive in America, over one hundred and fifty years before the Revolution, established a wider and more liberal franchise than had existed in the England they had left. There were exceptions—and early records are so scarce one cannot always be sure exactly what happened—but in the main, among the early settlers all males over 21 of "peaceable and honest conversation" could vote. The settlers arrived in tight groups all of whom knew each other. They shared common hardships, and they shared the vote. And, as we shall see, they also shared in their neglect to use it. The American voting lists of the 1660's use the term "freeman," anyone not a servant, and "freeholder," anyone owning property, almost interchangeably. Of course, totally excluded from this "liberal" franchise were women, Indians, blacks, Quakers, Jews, Catholics (in certain areas), ex-convicts, and usually servants. But the absence of a property qualification extended the vote far more widely in colonial America than in England or Europe.

In 1630 the Massachusetts Bay Colony, for example, allowed almost all "freemen" to vote. Initially the Virginia assembly granted the right to vote for the lower Virginia house to all inhabitants of plantations, specifically including both freemen without property and servants. When Maryland was first settled, not only was there no property requirement, but also no residency requirement. In England, political philosopher John Locke, drawing up the charter of the Carolina

Colony for one of its major investors, his patron, the Earl of Shaftesbury, tried to write the Colony's rules to "avoid a numerous democracy by dividing colonists into equally rigid compartments." In Carolina, the settlers tore up the notice of his restrictions.

Even in those colonies where land ownership was required in order to vote, the presence of plentiful land made such restrictions less odious in America than in England, where King and gentry owned all. William Parke, writing home to his family in Ireland from Pennsylvania in 1725, rejoiced that, though he had started as a tenant, he now had a 500-acre farm bought for 350 pounds saved by himself. He felt, he wrote, that America was "the best country for working folk and tradesmen of anywhere in the world."

So the country began. Then, as ever happens in human affairs, chance distributed fortune, energy, and ability unevenly. Some men prospered while others fell. Those who had gained moved to protect what they now held. At the same time, the less fortunate and the newer arrivals flocked to the frontiers of the colonies. So a clash developed between those with relative wealth and land and those with less, and also between the older settlements along the coasts and rivers, and the inland counties and towns. The numbers of those able to vote began to be restricted.

Virginia's disfranchising Act of 1670 disfranchised the freemen. In Massachusetts Bay the original Puritan settlers soon realized that acceptance of all freemen applications to vote would dilute their power and control. After admitting 118 new members to the vote in 1630, the colony's leaders moved to restrict future membership. From then on, no one could become a voter unless he was already a member of one of the colony's churches. It was not easy to become a church member. Of the 20,000 new settlers who arrived in Boston between 1630 and 1640, all of them Protestant and selected for trans-Atlantic shipment by their Bishop, only 1,148 passed this test. The Protestant divines obviously had stringent notions of the "good character" required for voting. Their maximum leader of the time, Governor John Winthrop, believed in a hierarchical society ordained by God. As for democracy, he "accounted [it] the meanest and worst of all forms of Government."

Religious qualifications limiting the franchise had been

enforced from the beginning in neighboring Plymouth, and after 1660 they spread from there and Boston to the rest of New England. An important root of these restrictions was the Mayflower Compact of November 11, 1620. The Compact, often cited as one of the cornerstones of American democracy, was actually a little sweetheart contract worthy of Boss Tweed of Tammany Hall. It kept the control of the Plymouth colony in the hands of the minority members of the Church of Leyden. All others who settled in the colony had to sign a piece of paper that gave them the right to pay taxes and keep quiet.

A neat twist on limiting the franchise was practiced in Rhode Island. There in 1636 Roger Williams, in his drive for toleration, had abolished the religious requirement for voting and declared his government "democratical." However, new settlers had to be admitted to the vote by a two-thirds decision of the original settlers. Williams, who knew the value of a misleading slogan as well as any of today's politicians, called this restriction: "the fellowship of the vote."

In addition to imposing religious limitations on the franchise, all the colonies, by the turn of the century, moved to enact or increase property qualifications for voting. In Maryland the upper house adopted a resolution that "the freeholders are the strength of this province, not the freemen." They then established as a qualification for voting the ownership of at least 50 acres. Massachusetts established a property requirement of taxable property worth 20 pounds a year. In 1669 Connecticut enacted its property requirement and New York followed several years later.

In 1654 the House of Burgesses of Virginia passed an act narrowing the franchise by taking the vote away from servants and from former servants who were now free. There was, however, much public opposition and the act was amended to return the vote of the new freemen, but to exclude servants. Then, in 1670, the issue resurfaced and the freemen were again disfranchised: "It is hereby enacted that none but freeholders and housekeepers . . . shall hereafter have a voice in the election of any Burgesses in this country [Virginia]." By the time of the Revolution, in order to vote in Virginia, a freeholder had to own 100 acres of unsettled land, or 25 acres of plantation, or a house and lot in an established town.

Those like Thomas Jefferson who wanted to do away

with property qualifications argued that the abundant free land made such restrictions meaningless. In a short time, Jefferson believed, all free men were bound to become property holders. All through his life Jefferson was ambivalent on how far to extend the franchise. Before the Revolution he wished the vote in Virginia to be limited to those who had served in the militia or paid taxes. He wrote his close friend Jeremiah Moore: "I should probably have proposed a general suffrage [for Virginia] because my opinion has always been in favor of it. Still I find some very honest men who, thinking the possession of some property necessary to give due independence of mind, are for restraining the elective franchise to property." Later he wrote to George Washington: "It is an axiom in my mind that our liberty can never be safe but in the hands of the people themselves and that, too, of the people with a *certain degree of instruction*" (italics ours).

The need to be a resident of a particular place for a given length of time developed as a peculiarly American restriction on voting. In England or Europe people, particularly ordinary people, simply did not move around in those days. But in mobile America those in power were fearful that vagabonds just passing through would saddle a colony with debts that the established landowners would have to meet. By the 1700's, some length of residency was required for the vote in all of the colonies, ranging from three months in New York to two years in Pennsylvania and Delaware.

In addition to legally established restrictions on the franchise, settlers along the frontier were denied the vote in other none too subtle ways. Colonial assemblies simply refused to create new counties or new legislative seats, or even to reapportion existing ones. Inland South Carolina had no representatives or judges whatsoever. In Virginia young Thomas Jefferson complained with justice that some 19,000 men in the Tidewaters were making laws and levying taxes on some 30,000 unrepresented men in the Piedmont.

Such political limitations went largely unchallenged because most of those on the frontier didn't give a damn about voting. As long as the Tidewater-dominated legislatures kept the Indians pacified, the roads open, and the taxes low, the frontiersman acquiesced in the theft of his vote. A fourth of the white population of the colonies was totally illiterate; another quarter were barely able to handle the English language. Ordinary people were used to the traditions and claims of aristocracy. They were content, even proud, to be represented by the great men of their colony—a trend that continues in today's America.

This description of campaigning in the *New York Gazette* of 1761 has a contemporary note: "A squeeze of the hand of a great man . . . a few well turned compliments, an invitation to his dining room . . . a glass of wine well applied, the civility and good humor of his Lady, the Drinking of a Health, inquiring kindly after the welfare of a family, a little facetious chat in a strain of Freedom and Equality, have been sufficient to win the heart of many a voter."

Not surprisingly, under such conditions and with such rules, refraining rose. By the time of the American Revolution the right to vote was more hedged about with restriction in America than in England, where, after 1720, practically all householders could vote. The emerging American aristocracy were moving to protect what they had gained, while the aristocracy in Britain were seeking to check the power of the King through a Parliament strengthened by broader suffrage.

In only one area was the American right to vote less restrictive at that time than in Great Britain. The English continued to make a property qualification the *sine qua non* of voting. But the colonies accepted payment of taxes or the existence of other forms of goods as an alternative, not caring if a man's wealth were derived from land or from business, trade, artisanry, or labor. Jefferson wanted to alter the Constitution of Virginia so that all taxpayers, albeit wealthy ones to be sure, could vote as well as landowners. In November 1775 New Hampshire abandoned the freehold qualification and extended the vote to all taxpayers. New Jersey enfranchised its growing merchant class by permitting 50 pounds worth of personal property to substitute for land. Connecticut, Delaware, Maryland, and Pennsylvania also set the limit at 50 pounds. Even in those parts of New England where restrictive religious covenants were in force a landless man could become eligible to vote by the payment of pew rental in a local church.

Still, in America at the time of the Revolution, the right to vote was highly restricted. By 1776, in all the colonies, a man had to have lived a certain length of time in a place, owned land or paid taxes, often quite high ones. In addition, in most of New England he had to belong to the right church. Of the population which we would today consider eligible to vote, 90 percent were legally disenfranchised for political or philosophical reasons. In Philadelphia only 2 percent of the population was eligible to vote. The famous fighting slogan, "No taxation without representation" implies, albeit *sotto voce*, that those not taxed—servants, bondsmen, women, the poorer freemen, and frontiersmen—did not count as voters.

Yet the sparse turnout among those few white, established males of sound religion and settled residence who were entitled to vote makes one wonder if the legislators need have been so restrictive. Only a handful of those entitled to vote exercised that right. Whether this was because of the physical difficulty of voting or because of sociological reasons is hard to tell. I tend to believe the latter. As with the positive apathetic refrainers of today, there was so much to do in colonial America that voting seemed unimportant to a great many people.

However, there were also major physical obstacles to voting. Election districts were large and the road network often nearly nonexistent. The letters of American settlers abound with complaints of riding two days to get to the polls and back. Polling times were uncertain, political information hard to come by, and the political parties did not exist. In such an atmosphere, refraining was an all-colonial-American fact of life. Voting was particularly low in New England. In Massachusetts, where only one man in fifty was eligible to vote, less than 2 percent of the eligibles went to the polls. In Connecticut less than one percent entered the booth. New York and Virginia had the best record on voting; 8 percent of the population of those states went to the polls. America was firmly founded on the right not to vote.

After the Revolution the low turnouts continued. Our early Presidents, from Washington, Adams, and Jefferson, all the way through Monroe, were all elected by 4 to 6 percent of those few who were eligible to vote. This is a fact that ought to give some pause to those who claim the size of the vote is inexorably intertwined with excellence in government. From the time of the Pilgrims to Andrew Jackson, voting turnout was not merely small, it was minuscule. And before the dramatic jump in voting under Andrew Jackson the physical restrictions on voting had remained almost the same for 40 years. Then, as today, it was not physical barriers that were keeping American voters from the polls. They were staying away chiefly because the political choices to be made then seemed unimportant to their lives.

The 55 delegates who gathered in Philadelphia at the end of the successful Revolution to frame what might or might not become a constitution realized they had to solve two problems. One: Who should vote? Two: For what? Their solution to the second problem—the bicameral chamber, the separation of legislative, executive, and judiciary power—has received the most historical attention. But the delegates themselves expended an equal amount of effort on the first question: Who should vote? Here they found themselves with little theoretical and no practical guidance. The question of who should vote had heretofore been considered as part of the balance between Monarchy, Aristocracy and Democracy. Lacking Monarchy and Aristocracy, how was the power of the vote to be controlled?

War is a great broadener of the franchise. Groups previously excluded from power often make up large numbers of those who die, or, if more fortunate, who pay for others' dying. The Napoleonic wars started agitation that led in 1832 to enfranchisement of the British middle class whose taxes had financed those wars. In our time, World War II, Korea, and Vietnam finally brought the vote to the 18-year-olds and abolished those restrictions, overt and covert, that had for so long kept blacks outside the process of American democracy. So the American Revolution created pressure to open the franchise to the recently arrived, the landless, and the frontier settler.

James Madison, later the fourth President, in his notebooks on the Constitutional Convention, recorded that "Symptoms of a leveling spirit . . . have sufficiently appeared . . . to give notice of future danger." He quoted Benjamin Franklin, who was less fearful of democracy than Madison, as remarking to the convention that "in time of war a country owed much to the lower class of citizens. . . . If denied the right of suffrage it would debase their spirit and detach them from the interest of the country."

The Constitutional Convention delegates were meeting

in a time of turmoil. The treasury was empty. Unemployed ex-soldiers were rioting for back pay. Parts of the frontier were in rebellion. Currency was fluctuating wildly. In addition to this turbulence around them, there was the example of England, where politics had become increasingly corrupt. This was the time of the ministries of North and Pitt, and the garish campaigns of John Wilkes and Charles Fox—all those excesses which have come down to us etched in acid on the plates of Hogarth and Gillray, and in the delightful ballad on how the Duchess of Devonshire put out in local taverns for Fox voters.

As witnesses to such turbulence and corruption, almost all the delegates wanted some restriction on the vote. There were few who agreed with James Wilson of Pennsylvania, who in 1720 had arrived in Maryland from Scotland and found himself unable to vote because of a residency requirement. Wilson now argued that restriction of "the rights of election in any shape [is] one of the most galling chains that the human mind can experience." His was a lone voice for broad suffrage.

Madison, on the other hand, spoke for most delegates: "In England, at this day, if the elections were open to all classes of people the property of the landed proprietors would be insecure." George Mason, delegate from Virginia, "conceived it would be as unnatural to refer the choice of a proper character for [President] to the people as it would be to refer a trial of colors to a blind man." Roger Sherman of Connecticut believed: "The people immediately should have as little to do as may be about the government. They . . . are constantly liable to be misled." Alexander Hamilton, with his usual succinctness, summed up the conservative side of the argument: "The voice of the people has been said to be the voice of God; and however generally this maxim has been quoted and believed, it is not true in fact. The people . . . seldom judge or determine right."

With practically all delegates agreed that stability required some restrictions on the franchise, the question became one of practical politics. How was the vote to be restricted? The political code words were "Republican" and "level." Republican was an attested "good thing," endorsed by the early days of the Roman Republic when the solid citizen farmer left his plow to do battle for freedom and honor. Level was an attested "bad thing" brought about by levelers in the last days of the Roman Empire when bread and circuses bought the ignorant and Caligula made his horse a Senator. For some reason Caligula's horse came in for a good deal of abuse. Poor dead Dobbin, surely he was not the worst legislator ever seen.

In trying to persuade their fellow delegates to broaden the franchise, Jefferson and Madison, who had slowly come round to the middle ground, argued that a large number of voters would protect the public interest and lessen corruption. Madison wrote: "The only remedy is to divide the sphere, and therefore divide the community into so great a number of interests and parties, that in the first place, a majority will not be likely at the same moment to have a common interest separate from that of the whole . . . and in case they should have such an interest they may not be apt to be united in the pursuit of it."

On the issue of corruption, Jefferson argued: "I believe we may lessen the danger of buying and selling votes, by making the number of votes too great for any purchase; I may further say that I have not observed men's honesty to increase with their riches."

For the future, Jefferson placed his hopes for effective voting on the spread of education. "Enlighten the people generally," he wrote, "and tyranny and oppressions of body and mind will vanish like evil spirits at the dawn of day." He often cited the constitution of Spain where "there was a principle . . . that no person born after that day, should ever acquire the rights of citizenship until he could read and write . . . . After a certain epoch [it] disfranchises every citizen who cannot read and write. This is new and is the fruitful germ of the improvement of everything good . . . [it] will immortalize its innovators." Jefferson's ideas on education as a voting qualification lay dormant until the great immigrant waves of the 1880's. Then they were exhumed in the form of literacy tests and enforced, not always evenhandedly, by many states until declared illegal in 1975.

The founding fathers solved part of the franchise arguments by having the House of Representatives elected directly by the people while the members of the Senate were appointed by the individual state legislatures.* The President was selected

---

*Admittedly it oversimplifies the issue to view the compromise on voting for the Senate and House solely in terms of franchise size. Southern and Northern interests, free trade and protectionism, small states and large all played a part. Human affairs are always complex. I am merely trying to stress the historical importance of franchise size in America.

in a fashion so complex that it broke down immediately after Washington and Adams. The problem of who should vote, however, proved too stubborn to be resolved. The deadlock was "solved" by returning the problem to the states with exhortations to liberalize the ballot with wise but deliberate speed. So the states have controlled who votes until today, though the Voting Rights Act of 1965, along with the toughening amendments of 1970, have finally strengthened the chidings of the Constitutional convention with the arm of Federal law.

Some states had begun to broaden their franchises during the Revolution; after the Constitutional convention, others joined the march, though in describing the progress emphasis would have to be on deliberate rather than on speed. At the Revolution's end only Vermont had adopted universal manhood suffrage. Kentucky, New Jersey, Maryland, and Connecticut reached this goal by 1818, though they still retained a form of poll tax. At the same time Delaware, Georgia, and North Carolina substituted tax payments for property qualification as a voting requirement—in part to assure white solidarity should the slaves revolt. Only Rhode Island marched backward, returning to operate under its colonial charter of 1663, a practice it continued until the Dorr rebellion in 1844.

On the Western frontier, the twin influences of an exploding population and the industrial revolution combined to produce a number of new states. Between 1816 and 1821 five such states plus Maine in the North entered the union. None of these required property ownership to vote. Such Western largess led to Eastern relaxation. New York, for example, extended the right to vote to paupers in 1821.

It is difficult to say what percentage of those eligible to vote actually went to the polls during the period between Washington's first presidency and the Jacksonian revolution. There were few voting lists, voting was largely by voice, and therefore fraud was easy and historical reconstruction difficult. Voice voting was not abolished generally until the middle of the 1800's. "I scarcely believe," said John Randolph of Virginia, defending the voice vote in 1839, "that we have such a fool in all Virginia as even to mention the vote by ballot; and I do not hesitate to say that the adoption of the ballot would make any nation a nation of scoundrels. . . ."

The meager figures obtainable indicate wide state fluctuations in turnout, in part because of local issues, in part because of franchise restrictions. In Connecticut, with its strict requirements for eligibility, only one man in ten voted, in Massachusetts about one in five. In contrast to the situation today, voters then were more apt to vote in local than in presidential elections. Historian Richard Hofstadter estimates the turnout then to be as high as 70 percent in an occasional hot local contest, whereas turnout in presidential elections held below 20 percent. In that period the presidential electors were still being chosen by the state legislators in two-thirds of the states. More important, the role of politics had not assumed the importance it held after the Jackson presidency. Ezra Pound's description of Jefferson's presidency is probably accurate, however bilious its view of one of history's great minds. "Apart from conversation and persiflage, how did Jefferson govern? What did he really do? Through what mechanisms did he act? He governed with a limited suffrage and by means of conversations with his more intelligent friends."

While the right to vote was being extended, slowly, to all white males, blacks were systematically being stricken from the election lists. (Females were to remain outside the system until 1869, when pioneer Wyoming risked letting them vote for governor.) Maine, New Hampshire, New York, Pennsylvania, and North Carolina as colonies had all permitted voting by free Negroes. In the 1800's this right began to be removed, and free blacks joined the ranks of enforced refrainers. After 1819 none of the new states admitted to the union permitted black voting until the close of the Civil War.

To deny the sociological, psychological, and philosophical limitations of that time which kept the vote from blacks and women would be ridiculous. But today, when Americans tend toward self-flagellation, let us recognize the glorious achievement in permitting all white males to vote. American universal male suffrage is one of the pioneering political acts of history. Periclean Athens never came close. Italy opened the ballot to all males only in 1919, the Netherlands in 1917. In Switzerland women could not vote until 1971. Today nation after nation, in the name of security or some other sophistry, removes from their people control over their own lives. America has many problems, including the major one that is the subject of this book, but we also have a few triumphs.

Andrew Jackson brought Americans to the polls. That much is sure though all the rest be lies. When Jackson ran against John Quincy Adams in 1824, only 355,000 votes were counted. Jackson was defeated when the closely contested election was thrown into the House of Representatives. A fuddy-duddy New York delegate, General Van Rensselaer, praying for guidance on the floor of the House (hardly the best place to get the word), saw at his feet a ballot marked Adams. Believing this to be a sign from God, he switched his vote to Adams. When Jackson and Adams faced each other four bitter years later, after one of the most vicious campaigns in United States history, indeed in any history, 1,155,000 people voted— a fantastic figure. This was an increase of 250 percent in four years, the greatest transformation of nonvoters into voters in American history. And it was accomplished without any change in the legal restrictions on voting.

Nor had there been changes in the voting laws when in his second campaign Franklin D. Roosevelt brought off the second greatest switch of nonvoters to voters, the increase then, however, being only 15 percent, from 38 million in 1932 to 45 million in 1936.

After Jackson brought them into the booth, Americans remained there. Four years after Jackson was elected to his second term, 78 percent of the voters turned out when, in 1836 in the midst of a depression, war hero General William Henry Harrison, "Old Tippicanoe," ran against Jackson's heir, President Martin Van Buren, "The Little Magician." This high plateau of participation held until the presidency of General Zachary Taylor (1848), when it started a gradual falloff.* The slide lasted until the early 1900's, at which time refrainers again outnumbered voters. Another surge of voting then occurred under Franklin D. Roosevelt, to be followed by our present, ever-hastening decline. In 1976 refrainers were within five percentage points of once again becoming a majority of the electorate.

What happened at the time of Jackson? It's uncertain, but it appears that there occurred a special combination of candidate, issues, and the vast reservoir of refrainers. This

---

*If political participation is accepted as the *sine qua non* of democratic excellence, our three greatest presidents were General Harrison, William Tyler, and General Zachary Taylor.

unique situation did not again arise until the time of Franklin
Roosevelt. And today, many, though not all, of the same
portents are gathered.

Jackson was the first president deliberately to reach out
to the refrainers—and since time and chance happeneth to all
men, he was most fortunate in having a large number of
refrainers to reach. Jackson used the emerging newspapers and
the new issues to make politics important. It was at this time
that de Tocqueville made his celebrated observation that an
American deprived of politics would be "deprived of half his
existence." Though Jackson used issues and patronage to build
a powerful Democratic Party, his coalition did not last. The
Whigs were able to run General Harrison, who represented the
Jackson virtues, and make a comeback. He who opens the
jackpot doesn't always rake in the chips.

Franklin Roosevelt, like Jackson, had a new reservoir of
refrainers to tap. The Nineteenth Amendment had given the
vote to women, but they had yet to vote in large numbers. Many
new immigrants and their children were entitled to vote, but so
far they had abstained for lack of interest. Finally there were the
blacks, though they were largely concentrated in the South
where they would continue to be denied the franchise until the
1960's. Also, like Jackson, Roosevelt was politically able to
combine a new medium of communication, radio, and new
issues to draw the refrainers into the booth.

In 1924 only 44 percent of the electorate voted. Twelve
years later, at Roosevelt's second election, 57 percent of the
electorate voted. The all-important fact about the Roosevelt
landslide is that, like Jackson's, it was made up almost entirely
of new voters. Only 10 percent of those who had previously
voted Republican switched to voting Democratic between 1928
and 1936. But among previous refrainers, Roosevelt achieved a
phenomenal margin. He reaped 80 percent of those voting for
the first time in 1932, and 85 percent of first-time voters in
1936. Further, the new voters chose the Democratic Party in a
ratio of 4 to 1. Voters don't switch parties. Refrainers join
parties and then, as voters, maintain their new allegiances,
changing the face of politics for decades.

By way of contrast, when in the elections of 1952 and
1956 the extremely popular General Eisenhower won his
landslide victories, the number of refrainers grew, from 38

percent to 41 percent. Eisenhower drew his votes from Independents and Democrats as well as from Republicans. Of those Democrats who voted for Eisenhower, few switched permanently to the Republican Party.

Similarly, the young and dynamic John F. Kennedy caused many Republicans and Independents to switch in sufficient numbers for his election. But though he momentarily checked it, he could not avert the rising tide of refraining. Perhaps Eisenhower and Kennedy lacked the right mix of issues and personality. Perhaps neither used the new medium of television to full effect. Perhaps, as history appears to indicate, there is a critical mass, close to 50 percent, which the numbers of refrainers must reach for great political changes to occur.

To return to history—between the presidency of General Zachary Taylor and the Civil War (1850–1860) there was a gradual decline in voting of around 10 or 12 percent. By the time of the Civil War roughly 75 percent of those eligible were voting. This high turnout created a problem for Lincoln and the Republicans. Though he and his party could persuade voters to switch to him, they had no large pool of refrainers to turn into permanent converts.

After Lincoln, the Republicans stayed in power partly through disfranchising voters in the South, partly by waving the bloody shirt in the North, partly with black support, and partly because they were the party of economic growth. These tactics helped the GOP to gain strength incrementally as new generations grew old enough to vote and assume the political habits of their fathers. But Lincoln and the Republicans never had the opportunity which was presented to Jackson and Roosevelt— and is present today—to build a new overwhelming political base.

Refraining rose rapidly after the Civil War, most markedly in the South. First, the Southern white voters were effectively disfranchised through measures passed by the Northern-dominated Congress. Then, as white voting power returned and carpetbagger governments were thrown out, the dominant Democratic Party effectively disfranchised blacks.

When in 1956 the civil rights movement began to press for black registration in Mississippi, only 5 percent of the blacks technically able to vote were registered. From our focus on refraining and its effects on America, the post-Civil War one-party South has produced two highly significant results. In the first place, until the 1950's, the percentages of both blacks and whites voting in the South were so low that they dragged the composite picture of the country way down—and affected greatly the image of the refrainer. In 1900 only about 38 percent of those eligible to vote did so in the South, while more than 80 percent of the eligibles voted in the non-South. When in 1924 only 43.9 percent of the eligibles went to the polls—the lowest turnout in our recent history—about 55 percent of those in the North voted as against about 23 percent in the South. At that moment the overwhelming majority of refrainers conformed to the stereotype. They were poor, white, or black Southerners.

But from 1960 on, the South has distorted the national voting statistics in a totally different fashion. Now voting in the North is plummeting—a 15 percent decline between 1960 and 1976. During the same period, Southern turnout has gone up from 47 percent to 48.5 percent with a dramatic rise in certain states: Mississippi, a 24.5 percent rise; Virginia, 15.3 percent; Alabama, 16.5 percent. These figures make the national decline appear less serious than it is. Today refraining in the South is far lower than in 1928, but refraining in the North is far higher than in 1928. The civil rights revolution of the 1960's has worked. The makeup of those who refrain has altered profoundly.

The North saw a more gradual post-Civil War decline in voting, which began in earnest after 1876. There was a marked lack of interest in politics. The business of America was taming, raping, exploiting, developing (pick your prejudice) the continent. Government finished a poor second against getting ahead. In fact, General Grant admitted to voting only once before he became President. One does not have to be a cynic to remark that in the period between Lincoln and Theodore Roosevelt politicians were generally a rather poor lot (always paying deference to those heroic and honorable exceptions such as Grover Cleveland). Civil War heroes vied for the vote, parades and banquets were organized, cash flowed, politicians wheeled and dealt, the growing newspapers thundered, and refraining rose.

Henry Adams, grandson of Jackson's defeated rival,

wrote of the period in his autobiography: "No period so thoroughly ordinary had been known in American politics since Christopher Columbus first disturbed the balance of American society." While General William T. "War is Hell" Sherman, ever direct, remarked:

> *Washington is corrupt as Hell. . . . I will avoid it as a pest house. . . . If forced to choose between the penitentiary and the White House, I would say: the penitentiary. . . . With universal suffrage and the organization of political parties, no man of supreme ability can be President. King Log is as good as King Stork.*

Trying to increase voting, reformers in the late 1800's took two entirely different approaches, one of which is anathema to reformers today. They tried to interest more people in voting, and they also tightened registration and voting requirements. This was the period of massive voting frauds. In the elections of 1868 and 1872, 8 percent more people voted in New York state than were registered. In 1910, when the New York City vote was challenged and recounted, 50 percent of the votes were found to be fraudulent. In New Jersey, glass ballot jars had to replace the wooden boxes to prevent vote stuffing. In Pennsylvania and Michigan, gangs of mobsters moved from polling place to polling place beating up the opposition and voting at will. Indeed so numerous were the instances of fraud that practically all voting statistics from this period are suspect.

The reformers introduced the secret, relatively tamper-proof Australian ballot, and later the voting machine. They forced lists of registered voters to be published, enacted stiffer residency requirements, established literacy tests, and instituted state supervision of voting lists. As a result the number of refrainers rose. Or did they? Or were merely fewer Lazaruses making their miraculous comeback from the grave each election day.

The heritage of this Progressive period in American history is important, both because we benefit from many of its accomplishments and also because many of today's reformers treat the threat of corruption at the polls as an old wives' tale. They dismiss as obstructionist balderdash the concerns over possible fraud in such practices as postcard registration. In their view, no Boss Tweed could possibly rise again. German militarism was pronounced dead in the 1920's. Yet temptation is still a lively non-partisan goddess, when she runs her tapered fingernails up your back and whispers, "This is your big opportunity," we all need some protection.

By 1912 the reformers had achieved another triumph, the direct election of senators. Until then senators had been appointed by the state legislatures. Following 1912 there were a series of lively local contests in which a great deal of money and political energy were spent. Yet refraining continued to rise. Not only were the new Senate races exciting, but both the elections of 1916 (Wilson versus Hughes) and 1920 (Cox versus Harding) presented important personalities and issues (whether to enter the war in 1916, whether to join the League of Nations in 1920). One would expect such a combination of national and local contests to arrest the surge of refraining. But the upward march of not voting continued.

This points to the difficulty of assessing the effect, if any, of political contests, particularly local ones, on long-term voting habits. In 1976 we saw hotly contested races in New York (Buckley against Moynihan) and California (Tunney against Hayakawa). In California there were important local issues on the ballot: authorization of nuclear power plants, limits of growth legislation. Yet in both states since 1960, the falloff in voting was ahead of the roughly 9 percent national average—a 16.7 percent decline in New York, a 14.4 percent decline in California. It takes more than an exciting local issue or candidate to light the fires of refrainers.

In 1920 a new group of voters battled their way to the franchise: women. They were led by a masterful coterie of thinkers, reformers, and politicians, including Susan B. Anthony, Lucretia C. Mott, and Elizabeth Cady Stanton. Like other fresh ranks of voters, they had also been helped by war. For example, in the decade between 1910 and 1920 the number of white women in clerical and sales jobs increased 103 percent and the number of black women rose 122 percent. World War I had created many more jobs for women, and, as a result, women became both economically and socially more free. Also, as usual, there was a political trade involved. The great experiment, Prohibition, was in progress. Dry politicians believed that the majority of women would vote dry and so help to keep the "wets" out.

As has happened each time a new group secured the right to vote—frontiersmen, immigrants, women, blacks, 18-year-olds—there was a time lag of ten years or more before the right was widely exercised. Therefore the first effect of women's entering the electorate was exactly the same as that of every other group, a dramatic rise in refraining. Not until the second Roosevelt election in 1936 did a majority of women cast their vote. At that time they, like all the other new voters, went better than 4 to 1 for FDR.

After 1925 we can be far more precise about who was and who was not voting. In 1924 Charles Merriam and Harold Gosnell published their study of not voting in the Chicago mayoral election of 1923, in which one-half of the eligible voters had stayed home.* In 1936 the University of Michigan began its study of the electorate and asked people to say in retrospect how they had voted in the Twenties. These are the studies, expanded in 1952 by the University of Michigan Survey Research Center, that form the bases for long-term assessments of voting behavior change. Coincidentally, the U.S. Bureau of the Census was extending its surveys and refining its data.

From all these sources we can form a reasonably accurate picture of the 1920's refrainers. In the South refrainers were primarily rural, poor, uneducated, and black, though a great many poor, rural whites also did not vote. In the North the dominant refraining type was a woman. Twice as many eligible women failed to vote as men. Also not voting were the foreign born or the children of foreign parents, as well as large numbers of urban blacks. As in the South, practically all the refrainers were poorer, less educated.

Attitudinal factors were also important in refraining, particularly feelings of political impotence. Merriam and Gosnell found that over and over "My vote doesn't count" was the reason given for refraining. Women, particularly first-and second-generation immigrants, felt they should not have anything to do

---

*It is impossible to overpraise this pioneer work which was done without a computer, at a time of limited statistical knowledge. Merriam and Gosnell polled 5,000 Chicago nonvoters and as a cross check another 5,000 voters. They also checked this mammoth sample (today's pollsters use 2,000 in all) against the voting lists to see if their respondents were telling the truth. In addition, they interviewed politicians, reporters, and social activists to refine and deepen their findings.

with politics. And their men agreed, often violently. Blacks cited feelings of alienation and a general disgust with politics. Interestingly enough, voting patterns were then greatly affected by the political organization within the precinct. In upper-class neighborhoods good organization brought more women to the polls, whereas in working-class neighborhoods it brought more men.

We are almost up to date. The Roosevelt revolution brought women, immigrants, and their children into the booth. Next, education took its own great leap forward aided by the "G.I. Bill" after World War II, that paid for the higher education of many veterans who would have never made college on their own. Yet contrary to all expectations, refraining was on the rise rather than falling as education increased. Then came the civil rights battles of the Sixties that, along with the Voting Rights Act of 1965 and the Amendments of 1970 and 1975, finally gave the Southern blacks in practice what they too long had held only in theory. Between 1952 and 1972 voting in the South increased by about 14 percent. Yet nationally, from 1960 on, refraining still rose. Finally the Twenty-Sixth Amendment to the Constitution lowered the voting age to eighteen. This new group of voters, like the women and frontiersmen before them, moved slowly to exercise their newly granted right. In 1972, 52 percent of the 18- to 20-year-olds indicated they did not vote. This occurred even though those refraining belong to the best-educated generation the country has produced.

"The future is a mirror where the past marches to meet itself." The first Pilgrims stepped off their wooden decks into the wilderness carrying with them the problem of refraining. The question of who should vote, who does vote, in what numbers, and why, was and is a particularly American problem. Refraining, too, has just celebrated a highly public bicentennial.

We live in a period in which all values, not just political values, are under question and attack. Families and political parties break up. The people divide toward the extremes. Landslides follow close elections. New elites rise and demand their share of the American pie. The world both flies apart and shrinks in ways as plain as the increase in our next lighting bill or the jet plane overhead. As part of this troubled time, refraining surges upward. Why? Who are the refrainers? How are they a product of our time? What is their future? And since so many of them are us, what is our future?

Having laid to rest the stereotype of Boobus Americanus, looked very briefly at categories of refrainers, and observed the refrainers' historical past, the time has come to bring the refrainers center stage, neither to praise nor blame, but to try to see them as they are. Then we may have learned enough to do something about their—our—problem.

3.
THE REFRAINERS: WARTS AND SMILES

Today's refrainers desert the booth because of attitudes they hold about life and politics. The data show very few refrainers who wish to vote but are kept from the booth by legal or physical restraints. Those who do not vote are younger, slightly more likely to be black, slightly poorer, slightly less educated than those who vote. But refrainers are not a different, left-out group of Americans decidedly poorer, black, less educated, worse housed than voters. By and large voters and refrainers attend the same schools, live in the same places, hold the same jobs, enjoy the same life styles; but they react to life in different ways. The reasons why refrainers don't vote are that they believe in luck rather than in planning, they feel their vote doesn't count, and they see no connection between politics and their personal lives.

In addition to these generalizations that we can make about all refrainers, it is equally important to stress that refrainers vary markedly one from another in the reasons why they don't vote. Those who do not vote divide into six major groups based on the dominant cause of their not voting: the Positive Apathetics, the Bypassed, the Politically Impotent, the Physically Disenfranchised, the Naysayers, and the Cross-pressured. The people in each of these groups usually differ from those in other groups in many ways besides their reason for refraining. To understand those who don't vote in their infinite and fascinating variety, one has the plunge into the details of the lives of each of the six types.

The Positive Apathetics. We are all familiar with that archetypal figure in literature and also in life, the man or woman who abandons private satisfactions, sacrifices family and personal pleasure to achieve political ambition. They have what might be called, in extremism, the Macbeth syndrome. We assume that highly successful politicians, indeed the successful in all walks of life, are liable to have mixed up kids and a troubled marriage. Among the refrainers a great many people (35 percent of those not voting) are the complete reverse of this picture. For these, the positive apathetics, the rewards of family and personal life, including often their jobs, are so great that they neglect their politics. Their lives are too full of other satisfactions for voting to matter. And they see no connection between the political system and their personal happiness and success. This apathy keeps them from the booth.

Apathy has been recognized as a basic attitude affecting political behavior since Bernard Berelson and his colleagues in 1954, produced the seminal work on voting behavior, *Voting*. The data for our study agree. Seventy-one percent of voters in our study were "very much interested" in who won the election. Only 39 percent of refrainers expressed such interest. Looked at in reverse, always an important check, 30 percent of the refrainers said they were "not much interested." Only 7 percent of the voters gave this answer. Traditionally it has been thought that one who expresses such apathy is Boobus Americanus again, the stereotyped "nonvoter." This is totally untrue. We found a whole group of refrainers bunched at the high end of the socioeconomic scale: happy, educated, well-off, but apathetic. They are the positive apathetics, and they have never been noted before.

The positive apathetics are strikingly different from many other refrainers. Indeed, in many ways they are more like voters than like refrainers. They are happier than other refrainers—in fact, as happy as voters. Eighty-three percent of the positive apathetics were either very happy or pretty happy, exactly the same percentage as voters, whereas only 73 percent of all refrainers said they were this happy. The positive

apathetics have a sense of political power. They feel more politically potent even than the voters. Sixty percent of the positive
apathetics indicated that if they were to vote their vote would
matter. Only 36 percent of refrainers in general felt this way,
and 55 percent of the voters.

The members of this group of refrainers are also more
likely to plan ahead than most refrainers. Forty-eight percent of
the positive apathetics said they planned ahead, against 37
percent of refrainers generally. They are much better educated
than most other refrainers. Thirty-one percent had some college or more, while only 24 percent of all refrainers had this
education. The positive apathetics are making good money
and are as likely as voters to live in the suburbs. Sixty-two
percent of the positive apathetics were making over $10,000 a
year, as against 55 percent of all refrainers in this economic
category. They are more likely to be male, 7 percent, than are
refrainers as a whole. They are also younger than other refrainers, 72 percent being 34 or under, compared to 61 percent
of all refrainers; and they are less likely to live in the South. They
are also slightly more likely to engage in community activities
than other refrainers, 32 percent against 27 percent.

Regarding political affairs, the positive apathetics are
definitely apathetic. In spite of their education, income, and
general alertness in the reinterviews, the positive apathetics
were the most likely of all refrainers not to have watched any of
the Ford-Carter television debates, though more likely than
many others to have been registered before. Thirty-four percent of the positive apathetics didn't watch a single televised
debate between the candidates during the 1976 presidential
campaign, as against 27 percent for all refrainers. Of con-
siderably more than passing interest is the fact that this group
contains a smaller proportion of Democrats than any other
group of refrainers except the bypassed, and a greater proportion of people who think of themselves as conservatives. Thirty-
three percent of all refrainers identified themselves as Democrats, while only 27 percent of the positive apathetics did so.
Twenty-seven percent of the positive apathetics felt they were
conservative, yet only 20 percent of all refrainers felt this way.

There you have them, by and large a group of young,
educated, happy refrainers who feel even more politically
potent than voters, who live where the affluent live, but who

don't vote. They refrain not out of bitterness or emptiness, as has customarily been thought, but because at present their lives are too full for the act of voting to seem important. "The world is so full of a number of things, I'm sure we should all be as happy as kings." The positive apathetics enjoy a bonus number of life's good things. They do live like kings—and like kings, they don't vote.

Typical of someone in this group is Ben O., our happy-go-lucky motorcycle repair shop supervisor who feels, "No matter who I vote for I don't think it will make much difference to me at all." At 23, making good money himself and coming from a family making over $25,000, he reports he is having a ball. He watched the television debates between Ford and Carter but "couldn't say that that man was right and that man wrong. . . . In a way I feel that what politicians do is none of my business. I don't vote in local elections either. It all seems sort of foreign. It's all media oriented. It's like selling toothpaste." But Ben O. is neither alienated nor uninvolved when he feels personally interested, as on questions about the environment, though here too he has trouble taking a side. He is concerned—for both his business and his recreation, trail bike riding—that "Carter is planning to close off the Federal lands to off-road vehicles." But he can see two sides to that too. "It's not my land." For him things are going too well to worry about politics.

Arlene S. lives with her salesman husband and two children in their own home in Irving, Texas, a suburb of Dallas. She definitely believes in planning ahead. "I kind of look forward to next month and plan when we're going home [to East Texas], vacations, simple things." She and her husband also do their financial planning together. Her husband, making around $14,000, has been with his firm for 26 years. They are quite happy with their life and look forward to retirement in a few years. "We'll be gone from the city. . . . back to the country where we came from." The country being Tyler, Texas, the rose capital of America. "The kids love it there, it's wide open, being out by themselves." She and her husband watched all three of the Ford-Carter debates and talked about the candidates together but neither of them could get really interested in the election. "I feel one is as good as the other." In the end her husband, who is a Democrat, voted "because he feels he should." Arlene didn't. "I never was much into politics." Arlene, who is 37 years old, never has voted, "Never did get into the habit."

On the East coast is Paul G., our 37-year-old soft drink salesman, Irish, a union member, a liberal—"the more I study the more liberal I get." Paul G. is a college graduate studying for his master's in his spare time. He makes around $20,000 a year and is quite happy. When interviewed, he was studying and his wife was out at the baseball game with one of their two children. The sea was breaking at the end of the dead-end street on which he lives in suburban New Jersey. In the previous week he had had two good job offers from which to choose when he got his master's. Right now, he pointed out, politics is just not his interest. Studying and working take up all his time. "Maybe though, when I finish all this, I will get interested." His wife teaches language arts at a grammar school. They talk about politics a lot but aren't certain that voting would affect their lives. Perhaps, he adds, voting is an illusion of choice, and voters are just like the people in Socrates' cave who thought they saw the real thing when all they viewed were the shadows; when we vote we don't have the choice that we think we have. Besides, he sees things in the country "as going okay." Far from cynical, he feels most politicians are trying to do a good job. "I have a positive view about so many things." He laughs. A true positive apathetic.

In south central Kansas on the Oklahoma border where the railroad tracks merge together to leap across the Arkansas River, 29-year-old Mrs. Muriel T., our woman who believes strongly in luck and is married to a railway engineer, expresses many of the same feelings. She is very happy right now. Luck has been good to her, her husband, and their four children. Whenever her husband gets a few days off from work, they try to go somewhere. That's what she was doing on the day of the presidential election, and that's why she didn't vote. She did vote for Nixon in 1972. "I don't think he should have gotten off. If he had been guilty, he should have got what was coming to him." But what Nixon did has not caused her to change her mind about politics or how she feels about elections. She has no trouble keeping registered. It's just that she might want to do something else instead of voting on election day.

Carlo N. in southern Texas feels the same way. He's our

high school graduate about to spend the summer in Europe, a
gift from his parents, before he goes to college. He and his
friends "have government and sociology in school. But we
don't talk much about it [politics]. We don't care much about
it. . . . The economy and what goes on is so big. . . . It doesn't
affect my life." Carlo N. is quite happy with his life. He says he
will probably vote sometime. "But right now I'm not too
concerned."

A fascinating subgroup among our positive apathetics
are those who avoid registering out of fear of jury duty. Many of
those who felt this way refused to give their names on the initial
survey. Others gave different reasons for not voting in the initial
interview, but informed us during the detailed interview, after
confidence had been established, that the real reason they
refrained was to avoid jury duty. This attitude was particularly
prevalent among small businessmen and farmers. Monroe M.,
a successful small businessman in New York, told us: "Frankly
to have to serve for one to two months on jury duty would be
impossible for me. I'm always in the middle of some highly
complex negotiation. I just can't afford to vote." Monroe M.
goes on to say that he doesn't feel that government is doing such
a bad job, all things considered, though taxes are too high and
too complicated. He doesn't feel that's going to change much
no matter who wins.

Mrs. Armand I., a farmer's wife in Centre County,
Pennsylvania, feels the same way about jury duty. Besides, she
would never want to sit in judgment on someone else because,
"I always feel sorry for the underdog." She adds that though
they don't talk about it much, "quite a few of my friends and
neighbors feel the same way." And they don't register to vote
for that reason. "I sort of felt that it was only me, till we got
talking, and they are all the same way." There are things that
she would like to see the government do, particularly helping
the small farmer and keeping land agricultural, not taxing it as
if it were going to be developed. But she just can't vote with that
jury duty hanging over her and her husband—not with a farm
to keep going.

It's hard to tell how many people are refraining in order
to avoid jury duty, because so many are so reluctant to reveal
this cause. The Field poll in California, with a justified repu-
tation for sophistication and accuracy, uncovered 5 percent of

their sample of refrainers in California who were not registered to avoid jury duty.

Also included in the positive apathetic category, though perhaps to be more accurate they fall right alongside it, are the overreporters, who say they vote when they do not. Our own previous work on these refrainers, augmented by Bernard Bookbinder's findings, indicates that the majority of the over-reporters are graced with attributes that match those of the positive apathetics: they are better educated, have higher incomes, are likely to know which political party they belonged to, and so forth. Had they reported refraining instead of lying about voting, they would have shown up as positive apathetics. This was confirmed when in our reinterviews all of those who now said they had voted (for Carter naturally), after reporting in the first interview that they had not voted, were positive apathetics. Also two reinterviewees in this category told us that although they had said on the initial poll that they had voted in 1972 or 1968, on talking to us at greater length, they guessed they hadn't voted then either.

Not unexpectedly, the positive apathetics lacked feelings of extreme partisanship. Forty-four percent of this group thought of themselves as Independents, 27 percent as Democrats, and 14 percent as Republicans. Here again, they were so satisfied, that the need for partisanship was missing. A sense of threat— "What is mine is about to be taken"—produces extreme partisanship. At this time the positive apathetics don't feel threatened.

Will the positive apathetics return to voting in the near future? You can't tell. None of the present palliatives being offered to make registration and voting easier much affects these refrainers. They are enough in control of their lives to register and vote if they so wish. Indeed, since the positive apathetics come from a socioeconomic milieu where duties and responsibilities are important, some of the proposals being advanced to make the process of voting easier may tend to drive them from the booth. Several of our positive apathetics objected that "voting is being sold like soap."

A detailed examination of what will and will not bring refrainers to the polls is part of the final chapter, but it's important to wave those battered red warning flags here. The positive apathetics are far, far removed from the traditional image of the "nonvoter." They are one of our three categories of refrainers who are most like the voters. Indeed the positive apathetics are more like the voters than are a whole group of voters who appear about to refrain. Of late this nation has tried to solve too many problems without understanding them— those highways we built that caused urban riots, and our famous "victory" in Vietnam. There is a marked danger, hence the warning flags, that we may pass legislation to increase voting turnout, only to see refraining take a fresh surge upward.

When the positive apathetics find politics more important than their present pleasures, they will vote—probably in large numbers. If they are brought to the booth by anger, they will react like any sleeping giant goaded awake.

The Bypassed. In this category, 13 percent of those who refrain, are people who most resemble the traditional image of the "nonvoter." The bypassed don't know if there are any differences between the political parties and they do not discuss politics or national affairs. They are not highly cynical about government, not because they have not been turned off by politics but because they have no political awareness at all. They are the bypassed because they have not just missed out on voting but also on many other parts of America: education, leisure, affluence, mobility.

The bypassed tend to live in the Deep South and the Great Lakes states. Only 17 percent of them thought you could plan your future, as against 40 percent of all other refrainers. They had lower incomes; 42 percent made less than $5,000 a year as against 20 percent of all other refrainers. Finally, 67 percent of the bypassed refrainers were female, as against 47 percent of all other refrainers.

This figure of 67 percent is dramatic because among all other groups of refrainers women vote at least as often as men. These bypassed women refrainers lack not just political awareness but usually feelings of self-worth and personal competence as well. Hopefully either the women's movement or some politician looking for new political resources will touch them and enrich their lives. When you interview some of these bypassed women they break your heart.

Significantly, the bypassed refrainers included only slightly more blacks, 4 percent more, than refrainers as a whole.

Eighteen percent of the bypassed refrainers were black, as against 14 percent of all refrainers. On questions of political impotence, 14 percent of the bypassed answered "don't know," as against 3 percent "don't know" for all other refrainers. These numbers again point up the great difference between the bypassed 13 percent and all other refrainers. Indeed, when working with statistics on who does and does not vote, it is often wise to run comparisons with the bypassed refrainers removed, for the bypassed continually distort the averages to skew the image of all refrainers toward the Boobus Americanus stereotype.

Mrs. Bea H., who is 29 years old, lives in an apartment in the western foothills of Appalachia and dreams of the day when she and her husband "if we ever do, get our own land. We'll put up a trailer or something. Then we'll be in the country. We like it here, but it's not country." Meanwhile her husband works as a maintenance man, and when he's out of work he watches the two children aged 2 and 3, while Bea H. works in a sewing machine factory. She doesn't vote because "you don't know who you can trust and who you can't." Besides, "With me workin', I'm really not too interested." She doesn't know which party she is for or how to register. She thinks you have to go over the mountains to the courthouse to register and that is a long trip.

Bea H. and her family have their ups and downs, but things keep working out. They get everything paid for sooner or later. She and her husband talk about politics occasionally. "About people gettin' more jobs and lower taxes. But when you get more jobs taxes have to go up. So it's kind of goofy." Her husband says "We ought to vote." But neither of them does. The election is such a long draggy thing, she points out, that you get tired of it.

Mabel D. lives in Corpus Christi, Texas, with her husband who is a retired bookkeeper. She herself used to work as a waitress but now, at the age of 60, she hasn't done that for 15 years. She has never voted. "My daddy didn't believe women should vote; it was for men." She says she is interested in politics and the election but would be embarrassed to go in and vote for fear that she might not do the right thing. "A woman 60 years old should really know how." So she takes her husband down to the polls and sits outside in the car while he votes. Her "daddy" was a farmer in Oklahoma, and she is really happy with the way life has turned out for her and her husband. She does wish she'd had more schooling—she left school before she had finished the eighth grade—then she wouldn't be so afraid of doing something wrong if she went to vote.

George U., 26 years old, is out of work right now and job prospects don't look too good. His mother makes about $6,000 a year as an order filler in a warehouse, and he is back living with her in St. Louis until things work out. He has some high school and is not too happy. In spite of all this he is one of the 14 percent of the bypassed who believe in planning ahead. "Don't try and shoot so far, not so far in the distance, or you get loused up."

He is not too interested in politics, "which is due to my general past . . . what I've been through." George U. was a depressed child and recently he has been having "a little trouble." He is hopeful that he is through that now and is brushing up to take the high school equivalency examination, after which he plans to go to Florida Bible College for four years. He is not sure what he will do after that. Is there any chance that he might vote in the future? "I don't see anywhere where it would carry a great weight. But it is part of my responsibility to society; to the country as a whole, the way it is run, and to myself." In the main he says he is feeling a little better about himself and the country. "I used to think that most politicians are crooked. But now I think that's an off-base statement."

While hardly thirsting for the vote, George U. seems more ready to enter the booth than most of the bypassed, particularly the elderly bypassed for whom not voting is a lifelong habit. A great deal must happen in every aspect of the bypasseds' lives, not just in their political lives, for them to vote. Things are not well with them. They have many lacks. In the face of their other wants the need to vote ranks low. To try to bring this group of refrainers to the polls is a worthy action no one can rightly be against. But if the goal is to refill the booth, and if our resources are limited, then to concentrate on the bypassed is the wrong approach. Other categories of refrainers are far more likely to return to the booth earlier and are much easier to motivate.

The Politically Impotent. If there can be said to be a hard core of refrainers, these, along with the bypassed, are they. Comprising 22 percent of all the refrainers, these nonvoters were categorized as politically impotent because their answers to all three of the political efficacy questions indicated feelings of extreme political powerlessness or impotence.* As might be expected with these feelings of extreme political impotence, they are also more politically cynical than the refrainers in general. Fifty-two percent of the politically impotent also expressed feelings of extreme political cynicism, against only 22 percent of all other refrainers. There are also a group of voters, 21 percent of the total sample, who have the same extreme feelings of impotence as these refrainers, and who, we believe, teeter on the edge of not voting.

While there are similarities between the politically impotent and the bypassed refrainers, what is more important is that there are profound differences. The politically impotent have shared much more completely in those bounties America offers today. Sixty-four percent of the politically impotent refrainers are making better than $10,000 a year, but only 29 percent of the bypassed are this affluent. Fifty-six percent of the political impotents have completed high school, while only 34 percent of the bypassed have done so. The impotent are far more likely to care who won than are the bypassed. They are also more likely to discuss their personal lives with non-family members. The two groups had very different political heroes: Senator Ted Kennedy for the impotents, President Carter for the bypasseds.

Of all our categories the politically impotent differ most markedly from the voters in their feelings about planning and luck. Sixty-six percent of the politically impotent refrainers believed life to be largely a matter of luck, as against 51 percent of all other refrainers and 38 percent of the voters. The

*In studies of the 1956 presidential election, the Survey Research Center of the University of Michigan found that an individual's sense of political efficacy did influence whether he or she would vote or not. More recently, both *The New York Times*–CBS poll and Bernard J. Bookbinder have also identified this group as an important source of nonvoters. The *Times* reported after the 1976 election that "while those that failed to vote were no more likely than voters to be alienated from the political system in an active hostile sense, they did differ markedly in that they tended to feel remote from government, to feel powerless and politically impotent."

disparity in these figures leads to an interesting question, which unfortunately we are unable to answer. But since interesting questions are often more fascinating without answers, here it is.

As life becomes more complex and as refraining rises, has the number of people who believe in luck rather than planning been rising? Or has that number remained constant with merely more and more people translating their doubts about the efficiency of future planning into refraining. Since no one to our knowledge has ever explored this question in ways that can be compared with our present survey, we can have no answer. Probably feelings of political alienation, and political impotence, arise out of general frustrations with life. Nie and colleagues discovered that between 1959 and 1971 the proportion of people's fears which were political doubled from 16 percent to 32 percent. A feeling that one's life is out of control, personally, economically, and politically, could lead to not voting. And these same feelings would lead to the conclusion that life is mostly luck. If one is putting out 200 percent, playing the game by the rules, and still losing, why is that? Luck.

This unanswerable question, "Is the number of Americans who believe in luck rising?" is a clue as to who the politically impotent are. Other clues include the fact that the politically impotent are not poorer than the rest of the refrainers but are grouped toward the upper middle of the middle class. Twenty-seven percent of the refrainers were making between $10,000 and $15,000 a year, but 36 percent of our politically impotent refrainers were in this income bracket. Fruthermore, these politically impotent refrainers were 14 percent more likely than other refrainers to be high school graduates who had not gone on to college.

They were much more likely to be older, in their thirties or early forties, than other refrainers; less likely, 33 percent versus 27 percent of all other refrainers, to know if they were liberal, moderate, or conservative. And they were more likely to have voted before. The fact that so many of them are middle-aged is alarming. Traditionally, the young have felt cut off from power. Now they carry this feeling into middle age.

Interestingly, these refrainers were also more likely to have voted for George McGovern than the rest of the refrainers who voted in 1972. Finally, the politically impotent refrainers were among the unhappiest people in our sample, as unhappy as those in bad health and the bypassed refrainers at the lower end of the economic scale. Twenty-six percent of all the refrainers said they were quite unhappy, 32 percent of the bypassed refrainers were quite unhappy, and 36 percent of the politically impotent. At the same time only 17 percent of the politically impotent classed themselves as very happy, while 24 percent of all refrainers felt that way.

Who are these unhappy, middle-income, middle-class, middle-aged people with extreme feelings of political impotence? Where do the confusing clues point? Here are some insights, based partly on this survey, partly on personal observation, partly on earlier surveys of voter attitudes. Blazes mark this group as largely composed of tradesmen, skilled workers, artisans, some of them working for themselves or as part owners or employees of small businesses. They are doing what their parents told them.They are obeying the system's commands, performing by both the letter and spirit of the rules. And not only do they find themselves unable to advance as they believe they should; worse, they find others coming up behind them.

Their parents probably voted Democratic. They consider themselves Democrats. When they have voted they usually voted Democratic. (Contrary to what you might expect, this group did not vote in large numbers for George Wallace, though the bypasseds did.) They can't see themselves voting Republican, but no one they hear is talking to their concerns or solving the political problems of their lives. As a result they feel their political lives are out of control. They feel alienated from a system to which they have given their all and which, they feel, now betrays them. I watched this group in Vietnam, the best of the middle class, sergeants and junior officers, doing "their duty." And what was their reward, forgotten by the public and the press? They got blown away first.

There have been suggestions that these politically impotent refrainers are that way because they get their political information from television. They are thus subject to an unchecked flood of conflicting images which they are unable to tune out or to sort out, and the confusion that follows leads to their alienation. The written press has also come in for its share of criticism in creating a climate of alienation. The charge is that news writers trivialize issues, make the political contest seem like a ball game rather than a battle of conflicting ideas. The charge is not so much that the press is politically biased, though this is also heard, but rather that the press is sensationalism biased, and the constant pounding of newsprint and electronic headlines turns people off.

"The press should consider whether it has contributed unduly to the profound disillusionment reflected in such attitudes. Is the news business, in its constant search for the startling, and the meaningful, distorting information in the process of relaying it? Are present techniques of political reporting the best and the fairest possible?" So wrote Charles B. Seib, the perceptive reporter who is the internal ombudsman of *The Washington Post.*

Though the press cannot be given 100 percent on its report card, nevertheless the data on these politically impotent refrainers, the second largest group in the sample, indicate a far deeper problem. As with the bypassed refrainers, the system is just not working for these people. And this includes the press. They don't see or hear "their kind of guy" on the tube or in the papers.

But unlike the bypassed refrainers, the politically im- potent have the knowledge, skills, and competence to handle their lives. In many ways they are doing quite well. Probably they are doing better, though not substantially better, than their parents. They have the capacity to vote. Many of them have voted in the past. Their parents voted. Remember, they fall in the age group where refraining is rising most rapidly.

Representative Don Bonkers of the state of Washing- ton, when he was chief registrar of his county, sent college students into every home and apartment in his area to register people. In about 15 percent of the dwellings they entered, they got chucked out. Most likely this group, the politically im- potent, were doing the chucking. They certainly were the group we had the hardest time reinterviewing.

Mrs. Sally F. is 48 years old and lives with her husband in southern Alabama, almost smack-dab on the Mississippi border. She is not a happy woman. They are way out in the country, in a place where Sally F. never intended to end up. Her husband, a retired Air Force sergeant, had wanted to travel around the country and look for the ideal place. But "he never did find it." So when his mother died they "sort of ended up here," and have lived here for four years. Besides this, though they are pretty well off, with $15,000 to $20,000 a year in income, she has to provide for her own mother, who is now in a nursing home. She felt that she didn't know much about the local politics or the community or how to vote. Her husband doesn't vote either.

Sally F. graduated from college in California, where she studied psychology and social science. As for voting, she doesn't feel it makes a lot of difference. Politicians go on their own corrupt ways no matter what the voters think or do. "Things keep turning up, all the things they get free. They get decent salaries and some of them are pretty wealthy to begin with. Those free haircuts—it all starts with little things like that. . . . It all starts with the county sheriff and goes to Washington."

Sally F. has never voted, something she blames on the fact that they were always traveling in the Air Force. She believes in luck rather than planning and would probably have voted for President Ford had she gone to the polls. She watched one of the television debates and doesn't feel there was much difference, if any, between the two candidates. Her feelings of political impotence extended all the way to our interview with her. When we thanked her, quite genuinely, for her time and help, she replied, "Well I don't think I've made much of a contribution."

Jane N. lives in Cincinnati, Ohio, on welfare at the edge of a low-income housing project. She has seven children, three grown. Her husband hasn't been able to work for the last two years because, they think, he has a tumor on his lung. Before that he drove a forklift. They live in five rooms of a house they are trying to buy but they don't have enough money to fix up the downstairs. One of her grown sons and his wife, who's expecting her first child, are living with her and her husband, and they contribute $25 a week to help out. Jane N., you may remember, said she didn't vote because she couldn't get anyone to stay with the children. "I've got some teenagers at home and they don't get along too good. I have to be a referee. They're fightin' all the time."

Jane N. classifies herself as a strong Democrat. Her father, who came from West Virginia and Kentucky, is a strong Democrat too. "He's always gettin' on us to vote." Her mother didn't vote though. She had seven children too. The last time Jane N. voted was in 1968, when she voted for George Wallace. Her husband didn't vote this election either. She is not sure if any of her grown children voted. They never talk about it. She said that she didn't like all that registering and reregistering; it was too much of a "hassle." She watched two of the television debates, didn't see too much difference between Ford and Carter, and didn't care too much who won. Her main hope right now is that they will get lucky and her husband will qualify for disability benefits. Then they would have enough money to fix up the downstairs of the house.

Frank D. is our 21-year-old plastic extrusion press operator in York, Pennsylvania, who says he probably won't vote unless Ted Kennedy runs. Married, with a two-year-old daughter, he makes close to $10,000 a year. All his family are strong Democrats and they all liked all of the Kennedys. "All the Kennedys know where they're going and things would have been different if Bobby Kennedy had been President."

Frank D. graduated from high school, believes in luck, and in politics considers himself a liberal. He is not as totally cynical about politics as many of the other politically impotent. He watched all three television debates and in the end felt that there was little difference between Ford and Carter. He also watched the David Frost programs with former President Nixon. He found Nixon "unbelievable, with all that responsibility, to say he's beyond the law." He feels that when Nixon was President "his head wasn't on straight," and mentioned an article in the local newspaper on Nixon by a psychiatrist.

He has been interested in politics since the high school civics course he took during the time of Watergate. He reads the local newspaper and a friend brings the *Philadelphia Inquirer* to work and he reads that too. His mother and father subscribe to *Newsweek* and he either reads their copy or picks up one on the newsstand. Though well informed about national government, and about sports, he's not interested in local government and doesn't feel his vote makes enough difference to be worth the trouble, "unless Kennedy was running."

Right now Frank D. is not too happy. The reason has to do with his work life, which is "mostly bad luck; but just luck." He has just missed out on a promotion to supervisor which would have meant more prestige and more money. He likes his job and "the only thing wrong is that there is no other company around York that does extruding like we do." He would like to work for DuPont but that would mean a move to Wilmington, and he's not too sure about that. He is proud of his work which is very specialized and which he trained himself to do. Now he doesn't know what will happen. So he will just sit tight and wait and see what comes up.

Would easier registration and easier voting make voters out of these three refrainers? At best, perhaps. All three possess the necessary skills to register and vote now, as do the vast majority of the politically impotent. Sally F., who has never voted, is a college graduate, Jane N. has voted once, Frank D. is articulate and politically informed. But all three think their vote doesn't matter. That's a political problem all right, but in the Aristotelian rather than the Washington meaning of the term.

The Physically Disenfranchised. These are the refrainers who wish to vote but are prevented from doing so for legal reasons, such as having moved too recently to register, having physical reasons, being out of town on election day, or suffering ill health. They make up 18 percent of all refrainers. Within this category, those too ill to vote, the "healths," form the largest subgroup, roughly a third of those physically disenfranchised or 6 percent of all refrainers. The physically disenfranchised refrainers receive a great deal of attention from politicians when they talk about bringing the "nonvoter" to the polls. However, the politicians completely mistake who is in this group, believing them once again to be the stereotyped non-voter. On the contrary, those physically disenfranchised (for reasons other than bad health) are among the happiest, wealthiest, best educated, most informed, most like the voters of all the refrainers. As for the "healths," most of them want to vote, know how, have often voted before, but just can't get a ballot.

The figure of 18 percent for the number of physically disenfranchised represents quite a bit of refinement and caution. We didn't want the data distorted by people who claimed they couldn't vote because they had just moved, or couldn't get a ride, or were out of town, when their actual reasons for refraining lay elsewhere. For example, a refrainer who said he or she did not vote for reasons of ill health but didn't see any difference between the political parties and discussed politics rarely, if at all, didn't make it into this category. In addition, those who said they couldn't vote for reasons of health had to be "very interested" or "somewhat interested" in following the election. Those who said they were physically disenfranchised for reasons other than health had to meet even stricter criteria. They had to be "very interested" in following the election. Admittedly, such criteria are arbitrary but they were not capricious. They evolved from our reporting and polling experience, the reinterviews, and voting behavior studies. And basically, when in doubt, we took people's word.

For example: Mrs. Jane E. in San Francisco, said that she did not vote because she was sick on election day. However, Mrs. E., 71 years old, is not and never has been registered. She has never voted. She did not know who she would have voted for. She believes in luck, does not know if there were any differences between Jimmy Carter and Gerald Ford, is unfamiliar with any politician's name other than Edward Kennedy. She is fairly happy and did not graduate from grade school. Mrs. E. may well have been sick on election day, but the chances are high that no matter how easy it was made for the sick to vote—and it should be made much easier—Mrs. E. would still be among the missing. Nevertheless, she was counted as part of the 18 percent physically disenfranchised because she said she was "very interested" in following the election. If she hadn't shown this interest she would have been placed in another category.

First a look at those physically disenfranchised for reasons other than health, 12 percent of all refrainers. This is a sizable body of people, but one a little too small to break down further statistically. Nevertheless, the data show they have quite distinctive characteristics. The most important of these is that, of all the refrainers, they are the most like voters. For example, they and the positive apathetics are happier and more likely to plan ahead than other refrainers. The physically disenfranchised are more trustful of government, better educated, and wealthier. They discuss politics often, they watched the campaign debates, are involved in community work, are more likely to be politically moderate than other refrainers, and a bit more likely than others to have voted for Ford if they could have voted. They appear to be a group of upwardly mobile Americans, many of whom had moved recently and who wanted to vote but were prevented by technicalities or job pressures.

Typical of those disenfranchised by a move were Bonaparte E. and his wife. Bonaparte E. has recently retired from the Air Force and moved from New Hampshire to Houston to practice his trade of paramedic. He is in the process of buying his own home and is happy. "We really like it here. This is a growing city. And the cost of living is much better in Texas than back East." He plans ahead, he likes his job. "It's an interesting job and you learn." He has voted in the last three national elections and also in local elections, even though the Air Force kept moving him around. "I haven't found it hard to register and vote in any one place that I have been." He hadn't found it hard to register in Houston either. He and his wife had already made a phone call about what they had to do. But they were told there was a year's wait before they could establish residency as voters in Texas. So Bonaparte E. and his wife missed the bicentennial election.

The move that disenfranchises can be a short one. John L. in Crawford County, Iowa, "Just moved one mile in the same town." Twenty-seven years old, and making just under $15,000 a year as an ambulance supervisor, John L. "follows politics as much as possible." His voice rises in exasperation as he talks about the last election: "I failed to get registered in time." He'd voted in both 1972 and 1974 and looked forward to voting this time, but he didn't realize he'd moved across a district dividing line and so had to register again. "I tried to get reregistered but it was too late."

Mary P., a college graduate with a new baby, found herself in the same situation moving from one part of Utah to another. It was two miles to where she had to register, and she had only a month in which to do it. She tried twice, and both times as she drove by the building there was no place to park. Mary P. is happy, married to a postal supervisor, has some college; she feels she has her life under control and a definite say in the running of the country. She does believe that life is more a matter of luck than planning. "A lot of things are a matter of luck, really. In the people I see around me that are really able to get ahead, they came into money from their parents. Their parents gave them things."

Mary P. points out that moving is one of the hardest

times for people. There is often a new child, or the family has changed jobs, the furniture doesn't arrive, finances are strained, the neighborhood is strange, the children have to be taken to new schools. At this time registration is an added burden. She has thought about this quite a bit and feels that there ought to be some way people can easily transfer their registration from one place to another, just as they change their postal address, particularly if the move is within the same state. There are many times when today's voters are ahead of today's politicians.

Those who gave as their reason for physical disenfranchisement that they were out of town during registration, or out of town on election day, have most of the same characteristics as those who had moved. Thus, again, they are more like voters than like other refrainers. They account for another 32 percent of those physically disenfranchised for reasons other than health. The chief difference between the out-of-town-on-election-day and the movers is that the out-of-town-on-election-day are overwhelmingly male while the just-moveds were much more female. This says more about our culture than about our voting.

Indeed, those who travel in America are so decisively male that Teeter once was able to help carry a local referendum in favor of fair housing by picking a day for the vote when the maximum number of males were out of town. Polling on behalf of a group trying to pass a fair housing ordinance in a large Michigan suburb, he found the referendum narrowly failing. The majority of women polled were in favor of fair housing, the majority of men against. The male majority was just enough greater than the number of females to defeat the measure. The vote was scheduled for a Monday, a day when, according to the data, most of the men were in town. A poll was taken that disclosed the maximum number of the town's males were out of town on the road on Wednesday. The election was switched to Wednesday, and as a result more women turned out than men and the ordinance just squeaked past.

Edward E., our 49-year-old, black, long-haul trucker from Los Angeles, is a typical traveling male. "Most of the truckers I know, they have trouble voting. . . . A lot of times they don't even have a chance to come home on election day." A union member who has voted before (in 1968 for Hubert Humphrey), Edward E. believes in luck but also is not cynical and feels he has some say in how political decisions turn out. "But the working hours are so bad." As Edward E. remembered it seven months later in June, he was on the Nogales vegetable run on election day and did not get home "till seven o'clock that night." Edward E. is definitely among the physically disenfranchised.

When we turn to those disenfranchised for reasons of health, 6 percent of all refrainers, we find two definite groups. One group appears much like the traditional "nonvoter" with little interest in politics or community affairs and, though slightly better educated than other refrainers, with strong feelings of political impotence. But there is a second very important older group who are very interested in politics, are involved in the community, have voted in the past, and now can't for health reasons. Fifty-eight percent of those refrainers who couldn't vote because of health were over 55 years old. Indeed, of all refrainers over 55, nearly 20 percent gave ill health as their reason for not voting; and these refrainers have every appearance of being habitual voters. They were also much more likely to have been registered than other refrainers. Almost certainly, one out of five of all refrainers over 55 today could vote if absentee ballots were not so difficult to obtain. This should be borne in mind in our discussion later in the book of a number of low-cost but effective ways to help end the rising curve of refraining.

An example of a voter disenfranchised for reasons of health is Thomas B. of Springfield, Vermont, a taciturn, 58-year-old New Englander with a dry wit. Thomas B. always has voted in the past. "I voted this spring locally. And I expect to vote in the next national election—if I'm still around." He lives by himself in a small town and likes politics, particularly local politics. "The local races are more important." But he was in the hospital on election day. When reinterviewed he was out and feeling much better. "We do have an absentee ballot, but it was too difficult to get." Thomas B. believes in planning ahead and feels he has control over his life, though not as much as he used to. He has all the characteristics of a voter. A political system that does not take into account ill health had caused him to lose his vote.

The same problem of health took the vote of Mrs. Louella D., who has been paralyzed for three years. Her illness hit her one night after she'd been working all day at a laundry press, and now she must use a walker. She watches the television news and wanted to vote for Carter because he was a Democrat and a Southerner, "one of us." Louella D., who is black, lives in a small Arkansas town on the Mississippi River just across from Tennessee. She gets around indoors pretty well, does her own cleaning and cooking, and the neighbors help out. "I've got nice friends here." A conservative, Mrs. D. left the Democratic party to vote for Nixon in 1972. Now she feels "bad, real bad" that she couldn't vote for Carter. Though Louella D. has definite feelings of powerlessness and, unlike Thomas B., believes life more a matter of luck, she is up on the news and has definite opinions about a number of political figures and issues. She is another of the 6 percent whom ill health transformed from voters to refrainers.

Of those 12 percent of refrainers physically disenfranchised for reasons other than health, 34 percent (or 4 percent of the total number of refrainers) had the type of trouble registering or voting typically associated with voters kept from the polls by hassle. This rather small group will certainly be helped by many of the measures being discussed to make registration easier, though the vast majority of the physically disenfranchised will hardly be helped at all.

Ella W. is someone physically disenfranchised in ways that prevailed until the middle Sixties and that are still occasionally found today. Thirty-nine years old and separated from her husband, Ella W. lives in a small, pleasant Pennsylvania town just off the throughway west of Pittsburgh. She has many of the characteristic attitudes of a voter. Though she believes in luck, she feels politically powerful and is involved in efforts to make her town better. She voted for Humphrey in 1968. Humphrey along with George Wallace and Edward Kennedy are her political heroes. She went down to the polls on election day to vote for Jimmy Carter, whom she liked, and then discovered that because she had not voted in 1972—she didn't like either George McGovern or Richard Nixon—she was no longer registered. She knew some of the people checking registration; they knew her and knew that she was living where she said and that she had lived there for several years. But the law was the law and she could not vote. This annoyed her. "I would have voted. I wanted to vote. I think you should have one-time registration if you don't move from the township."

The technicality that disenfranchised Ella W., the removal of previously registered voters from the rolls, or "purging the rolls," is a complicated and tricky business. The methods used vary from state to state. In some states, such as New York, where registrars like to point to large numbers of registered voters in their districts as proof that they are doing a good job, the lists are practically never purged. People who have moved, died, gone to jail, or become missing persons continue to grace the rolls. In other states, such as Washington, the rolls are rigidly purged of those who haven't voted, and residency records and death notices are checked. It's a difficult problem. While I was going to college I lived by myself in a small, two-room apartment belonging to one of the city's leading politicians. Glancing at the rolls as I arrived to vote late one election day, I was surprised to discover nine other people living with me, and all but one of them showing commendable democratic zeal, had beaten me to the polls.

While ease of registration is usually cited as the vital ingredient for increased turnout, that's just part of the problem. Ease of registration maintenance, along with reliable record keeping, is equally important but, not being as exciting an issue, is too often neglected.

Undoubtedly with better registration and voting procedures that are designed with the true physically disenfranchised in mind, many in this group, people like Ella W. and Thomas B., will vote. But in this group of refrainers people still stress that what they really want is better candidates. Even with a system designed by the archangel Gabriel himself to help each soul to the polls, some of the physically disenfranchised will remain refrainers. Still this is the group of refrainers most like voters. With the proper help, the physically disenfranchised are the refrainers most likely to be in the booth next election.

The Naysayers. These form a fascinating group of refrainers, seldom noted before. It is the pride of the naysayer not to vote. They are verbal "no" people hurling down boulders on elections and candidates. While so few in number—6 percent of all refrainers—that statistical descriptions are impossible, they are highly visible, often intelligent and articulate. The naysayers placed themselves in this special category because on the questionnaire they stated that they did not vote because they had deliberately chosen neither to register or to vote. For the naysayers, not voting is a highly conscious act they are willing to defend at length.

Examining the naysayers both in their survey answers and in the reinterviews, one can make some interesting generalizations about them. They are better educated, more likely to discuss politics, and usually wealthier than other refrainers. They are also among the most highly cynical of all refrainers and, along with the politically impotent, the most inclined to believe life largely a matter of luck. They were also very likely to have watched all three television debates, and they tended to classify themselves as political liberals or moderates. They are definitely more likely to be male than other refrainers, are usually younger, and are somewhat less likely to live in the South. They were apt to say "no" to things other than politics. Few of them take part in community activities. In our reinterviews the definite, rational nature of the naysayers' choice to refrain came through strongly.

No one reason dominates the naysayer's decision to refrain. For some it's philosophy, for some religion, for some a bad experience with national or local politics. They have worked for a candidate or issue that lost and now their attitude is "a plague on both your houses." Undoubtedly for others a loud "no" is their habitual posture toward life.

Haynes Johnson of *The Washington Post* became fascinated by the naysayers in his 1976 travels about the country. "They usually can tell you quite specifically why they will abstain this Tuesday," he wrote. "For many the decision comes after careful deliberation. They aren't voting for lack of thought."

In talking to Haynes about this group that intrigues us both, he developed the theory that many of them were "Hamlets." They talk and think about politics endlessly, but feel such guilt about their own positive responses toward power that in the end they don't vote. I find there are two further types. One is the highly intellectual person whose commitment it is to have no commitment. This man or woman can see three sides to every question and, like the medieval scholastic's donkey who starved to death equidistantly from two bales of hay, they end up by refraining. Then there are the yogis who keep themselves unspotted by the world. Unless they can have perfection, they will not participate in love affairs, in shaping children, or in entering the wicked world of the voting booth.

An archetypal naysayer is a man we did not interview, Rabbi Howard Singer of West Hartford, Connecticut. Rabbi Singer was so sure that not voting was the best course to follow in 1976 that he wrote an article for *The New York Times* to prove it. He compared the nonvoters to "the noblest spirits in the Middle Ages. Thinking the world beyond hope they retreated to monasteries. . . . I can't vote for either of the two mediocrities offered for our approval . . . I won't feel guilty about it. A conscious rejection of a corrupt process and a fake choice is morally preferable to flipping a coin."

For three respondents—Elizabeth U., Mims T., and Paul T.—the reason for their naysaying is religious.

Elizabeth U., the secretary who lives in the Houston suburbs, believes in planning and watched all three debates. She can identify and talk about all the major national political figures. She gives her reason for refraining as follows: "I believe the system will be changed by God's will. To get really involved now is wrong. . . . My parents didn't vote. They feel the same way I do. So do my friends." She is certain that in refraining she has made the correct choice. "It's my decision what to do," she says. Note the positive choice. Elizabeth U. is a naysayer.

Mims T. is the retired construction worker who lives beneath the Iron Mountain range in southern Virginia. He has voted in seven elections and can recall each one. His parents voted and he remembers that well too. Now he feels: "I don't think I ever will vote again. . . . In the beginning we were a Christian people, or we claimed to be; and Christian people should not fool with what politics has come to be." He doesn't think anything would make him change his mind. What politicians do "doesn't affect me."

Paul T. lives with a group of religiously committed people like himself in a large house near the Connecticut shore. He avoids the word "commune," saying, "We are a group who feel the same and have settled together through commitments." He is 25 years old, has had some college, and is now working in a print shop. In 1972, when he had just turned eighteen, he voted for McGovern. "I was not that concerned about the country but I just voted because that was the thing to do. . . . Then I got into a religious movement, so I was not concerned about politics at the time this vote [Ford vs. Carter] was taking place. . . . Basically what I feel is this: no matter what happens the country will go a certain way, no matter what I do." He pauses and then adds: "I don't know how much time this country has left. I wouldn't say more than fifty years. . . . God has a plan for me and I don't have to be worried." He does not know if he will ever vote again. "I have to get my own personal life, my own religious life together first, before I decide."

For Gloria E., James W., and Emma E., the reasons for their naysaying are political. They share interesting insights and angers about national and local conditions.

Gloria E. is the woman who works in city government on central Florida's Gulf Coast. Her disgust at both local and national politics causes her to refrain. "I work in the city government and I can see how things have changed there until nothing is done with people in mind. The manager in our [local] government has taken away our step increase. White-collar workers don't even have a union. We are like working in slavery. . . . Politicians are all on an ego trip. . . . Nationally you have Watergate. What more do I need to say? When they are not interested in you, you lose interest in them. . . . When you see the deals in city hall, the behavior of the big unions, and the newspapers and power brokers, one hand wiping the other, why vote?"

As with Gloria E., firsthand experience of local politics has brought James W. to the ranks of the naysaying refrainers. James W. has just finished high school in Indianapolis. He comes from a middle-class family and considers himself reasonably happy. He is only mildly cynical about the government, has opinions about all the national politicians, his favorites being Carter and Kennedy, and he believes in planning ahead. He told us he could talk at length about what was wrong with politics: how there were bureaucrats everywhere, how most Washington politicians were more interested in getting votes than in listening to or helping people, how the state's famous senator, Birch Bayh, is a redneck. As an example of how the bureaucrats harass people, he talked about the

Internal Revenue Service regulations: how complex these were and the amount of time a small businessman had to spend filling out forms.

Then James W. got to the nut. He and his family are registered as Republicans "but we're all really Democrats." However, his mother works in the state house and the only way she could get her job was to register as a Republican. "That's real discrimination." It is the sort of thing that makes James W. doubt that he will vote in the near future.

Emma E. is the native Missourian who is waiting for another Harry Truman. She now lives outside of Erie, Pennsylvania, having just been forced from her home of 23 years by neighborhood crime. Emma E. hasn't voted since back in the days of Truman and Eisenhower. She thinks both political parties have become the same: they exist to get into office and give their friends jobs. This is particularly true "of the crooks they've got in Pennsylvania."

She watched all three of the Ford–Carter television debates. "And let me tell you, I think those debates were a lot of hooey. . . . I think Nixon should be put in jail with the rest of them." She doesn't think that there is much chance of her ever voting again. "It's not just politics, it's everything. Everything in the country is just all messed up." She pauses a moment and adds that she might vote if one candidate was "for something really radical, like a war or something." Like the other nay-sayers we polled, Emma E. does not feel bad at all about not voting, not with the candidates they have today. "If somebody could come up with another like Harry Truman I might go back to the polls."

Alonzo W., is a Mexican-American in whom politics and philosophy have combined to make him a refrainer. A 37-year-old with some college, he helps administer a technical school within five miles of the Rio Grande. Up to the last election Alonzo W. not only voted in all national and local elections, he also worked hard on community problems, which he still does. But he is upset by the whole thrust of today's America, including President Carter, whom he sees as "just treading water with no real programs."

Among Alonzo W.'s concerns is the energy crisis. "We don't have the resources to even evaluate what the true situation is." He also worries about the increasing cost of social security, as well as about the future of young Mexican-Americans in his area—the school dropouts, their low education rates. He is disgusted with local politics, the wealthy Mexican-Americans who pretend to be friends of the people but are just front men for even wealthier interests that are controlled by Anglos. "One of the worst things is the judicial system we have here." Then there is the illegal aliens problem, people who sneak in illegally, claim services, go back to Mexico, and make it tougher for Americans like himself. On top of all this are the problems of financing his children's education on his salary of $18,500 a year.

He sees no one interested in the problems of those who are Mexican-Americans like himself. In desperation he voted for Nixon, though he was a Democrat. Watergate followed. "So now there is a big question mark. It makes me wonder if anything I do can be effective. . . . I may give it one more try. And then that's it." With his social insights, his cares for his people and his political work, Alonzo W. represents the idealist turned naysayer. Only for him it wasn't the first defeat that produced the change, it was the hundredth.

With their intense, almost religious convictions about not voting, the naysayers are not going to enter the booth as a result of any of the "reforms" now contemplated. Indeed, they probably will be among the last of the refrainers to vote. They need an exceptional combination of candidate and issue to break through the crust of their suspicions. Even then, to change them will take time. And those naysayers for whom refraining fills a deep psychological need, the Hamlets and the yogis, will never enter the booth.

The Cross-pressured. These refrainers do not vote because they feel pulled first toward one party or candidate then toward another. They make up 5 percent of our refrainers, so again it is difficult to make statistical generalizations about them. Many social scientists, sophisticated politicians, and reporters, including myself, had believed this group of refrainers to be larger than it proved to be. Perhaps it was larger once, but as the ties that bind Americans to their separate pasts, cultures, and families begin to fade, cross-pressures on the voting decision may also be fading.

Bernard Berelson and colleagues in their 1954 book

Voting are usually credited with being first to identify the cross-pressured. They found that cross-pressure usually resulted from socioeconomic causes. A lifelong Democrat suddenly making more money finds himself in a neighborhood and among friends who are largely Republican. Or a liberal Jewish girl marries a conservative Southern WASP and they both stop voting.

Others see cross-pressure as more likely to operate at the level of conscious political attitudes. For example, one of the ironies of the 1976 election was that between the two major candidates for president, President Ford was in many ways the more liberal. This inversion produced conflicts during the election. There was conflict for liberal Democrats who wanted to vote for the most liberal candidate but had trouble voting Republican, especially with Robert Dole as Ford's running mate. There was conflict also for conservative Republicans who preferred the Southern conservative Carter but had trouble voting Democratic, particularly with Walter Mondale on the ticket. The result in both instances, cross-pressure and not voting. When Carter began to shift his position leftward, the cross-pressures began to operate on conservative Democrats. Interviewing potential voters two months before the election, *The New York Times*–CBS poll found that the greatest number of those who said they had not yet made up their minds were more conservative than average, had voted for Richard Nixon in 1972, were blue-collar, had preferred Ronald Reagan, were more likely to be female, and were also more inclined to distrust the government. This set of characteristics sounds like a melange of the politically impotent and cross-pressured categories.

The cross-pressured refrainers we studied come across as follows. Like the naysayers and the physically disenfranchised, they are far better educated than the average refrainer. They are apt to be younger than other refrainers and also more likely to live in the West. Furthermore, they are more likely to live in the suburbs than are voters. As for happiness, feelings of political power, and income, here they are about on a par with the other refrainers. They have a great deal of political knowledge, were very likely to have watched at least one of the campaign television debates, and are more apt to take part in community work than other refrainers. They are slightly more likely to classify themselves as political liberals, but much more likely not to be sure how to classify themselves politically, or to be certain whether they are Republicans, Democrats, or Independents. Obviously, they are cross-pressured about all aspects of politics.

One is left with the impression, though it comes more through feeling and reinterviews than through whatever iron logic statistics possess, that we are dealing here with a group of refrainers many of whom until recently were voters. Perhaps many of them were among those voters who had recently experienced "betrayal" or felt irrelevant or ignored.

Lurine K., a 39-year-old nurse who lives 15 miles east of Phoenix and whose hours in the operating room are "dumb, just plain dumb," and Betty Ann D. in Kingston, Pennsylvania, both gave answers that indicate conflict. Both are happy, in their thirties, middle income, watched the TV debates, take part or have taken part in community activities, and feel reasonably powerful and only moderately cynical. Betty Ann D. works in a sewing maching factory and sells Tupperware to make extra money. Her husband is a vending machine inspector. Both women and their husbands used to vote but "have sort of got out of the habit." Lurine K. says she is proud to be a conservative Democrat; Betty Ann D., considers herself a moderate Democrat. Mrs. K. believes in planning, Mrs. D. believes in luck.

Both are interested in current events. Betty Ann D. "had a good current events teacher in high school who got me interested." Lurine K. "used to be more interested in politics when the kids were younger." But they both find it hard to choose the better candidate. One senses they are right on the edge of voting but not quite. "By the time we made up our minds it was too late to register," says Betty Ann D. Besides, she stresses, she and her husband really think they should vote "and will vote in the next election," but this time they were busy repairing their house, which was damaged in last year's hurricane and floods.

Lurine K. feels the same way. "My mother voted. I know a person should take time out to vote, they really should. These are things they really should do." But it is so difficult to choose. "If you are not sure which is the best one it is really hard. . . . There's been a change in politics. . . . If I didn't feel he was the right man I wouldn't want to put my name on the vote."

On the Pacific coast Clare H. in Citrus Heights, California, illustrates the difficulty of fitting refrainers into categories. She is intensely cynical about the government and has strong feelings of political impotence, though she definitely believes in planning. She is a Democrat, reasonably well off, 29 years old with two children, aged three and four. She had just quit a good job with a firm of brokers to be able to spend more time with her children because a feeling of family is important. She and her husband are very happy. Her husband had been going to night school for the last three years and on graduation he got a major promotion and was made vice-president of the local branch of his bank. Mr. H., also a Democrat, didn't vote in this last election either. Yet Clare H. has been strongly active in local affairs. When she lived in Ohio she organized her town and blocked a move by the state to try to annex certain town functions.

In the original interview Clare H. gave as the reason she and her husband had not voted the fact that they recently moved. Since they had voted in the last three elections, this seemed logical. But in the follow-up interview Mrs. H. said that they had been living in California for close to a year before the election. Her real reason, she guessed, was that both she and her husband could not make up their minds who they were for. They used to be Democrats but now "lean more to the Republican or Independent." She classes herself as a conservative. Her political heroes are Nelson Rockefeller and Teddy Kennedy. She voted for Humphrey in 1968, Nixon in 1972. Now she's refrained. She thought that Carter was "too new." At first her husband was going to vote for Carter, "then he changed his mind."

None of the three refrainers just described has deserted the booth for lack of information. They are successful middle-class people with settled homes and their lives in order. They follow politics; they know the joys of civic responsibility; their parents voted, and they want to vote. Yet they can't make up their minds. They and their spouses appear all to be in the same category: cross-pressured refrainers.

Traditionally one of the ways to help someone in conflict is to make the decision easier for that person. Easier

registration would undoubtedly help some of the these refrainers. In particular, those who make up their minds late, as
many do, would be helped if registration were permitted closer
to election day. Or they might register earlier if there were a
postcard form in their home. But most of the cross-pressured
would still refrain. The native hue of their resolution is sicklied
o'er by the pale cast of political thought. Not the system's
mechanics but their personal and political conflicts are the
cause of their refraining.

That should really be the end of the categories. But
there remains a large group of people vitally important in the
future rise or decline of voting. The key role they will play
dictates their inclusion here even though they do not make up
any percentage of the sample of refrainers. Those in this
category still vote. They have not deserted the booth. But all
through this book the theme has been reiterated, that refrainers
and voters are very much alike. And this particular group of
voters has more of the characteristics of refrainers than many
refrainers themselves. We call such voters Vergers—they are on
the verge between voting and refraining. We have described
those refrainers who probably will be the first to vote. These are
the voters who probably will be the first to leave the system;
these vergers of 1976 are the refrainers of 1980.

In their monumental 1960 work, Angus Campbell and
colleagues acknowledged the existence of such voters with the
words: "The deviant voter, the man we would expect *not* to vote
but who does vote is as difficult to explain as the deviant
nonvoter, who would be expected to vote but does not."

Who are these voters, and why do they continue, at least
for now, to fill the booth?

The voters who look most like refrainers are the 21
percent of all voters who showed extreme feelings of political
impotence. Imagine the rise in refraining if even a small
portion of these vergers do not vote in 1980. The vergers were
placed in this category because their answers to all three
questions of political efficacy showed extreme feelings of political impotence. We then found that in many other ways they
were more like refrainers than voters. For example, vergers
were even more cynical about politicians and government than
refrainers, let alone than other voters. Seventy-one percent of

them fell at the high end of the cynicism scale, as against 58 percent of the refrainers and 43 percent of the other voters. They are as unlikely to discuss politics as refrainers, like refrainers they don't do community work, and they are making even less money than the average refrainer. Only 51 percent of the vergers made over $10,000 a year, whereas 55 percent of the refrainers made over this figure, as did 70 percent of the other voters.

Furthermore, the vergers were less well educated than the other voters, were less inclined to talk about family affairs, and were significantly older, 41 percent of them being over 55 while only 29 percent of the other voters were this age. Interestingly, the vergers made up their minds to vote earlier than other voters. Thirty-one percent of them had decided to vote even before the first primaries, whereas only 23 percent of the other voters felt this way—a perfect illustration of the mystic, irrational strength of the voting act. Vergers and refrainers were also identical in the proportion of them who were black, 14 percent. They were also alike in not being as happy as the rest of the voters. Twenty-six percent of the refrainers were not too happy, 24 percent of the vergers were not too happy, whereas only 13 percent of the rest of the voters were not too happy.

However, the vergers and refrainers differed in two interesting ways. The refrainers were more likely to live in the South, 36 percent, than the vergers, 29 percent. The vergers, on the other hand, were somewhat more likely to live in the Midwest.

And once again the almost magic dividing line of plan/luck held true. Forty-eight percent of the vergers believed you could plan life ahead, while only 37 percent of the refrainers believed this to be true. Forty-nine percent of the vergers believed in luck (4 percent answered they didn't know), a number equivalent to 13 percent of all voters. This 13 percent form a group who are highly politically impotent, believe in luck and yet continue to vote; even though they are more like refrainers than most refrainers. Undoubtedly many of these people did not vote, particularly the younger educated ones, but merely said they did. Still that leaves a sizable number of voters poised not just on the verge of refraining, but with one foot already over the edge.

These vergers, particularly the older ones who began voting with the Roosevelt coalition—either for or against—and who have recently become frustrated with the system, are held in the booth by waning habit rather than conviction. Forty-one percent of the vergers are over 55 years old. They have always voted. They voted in 1976 and the indications are that they will continue to vote. Political habit, like a long lasting marriage, can absorb quite a few shocks before it flies apart. But what of those under 55? Will the dramatic strength of the voting bond hold for them? The sharp rise in refraining in the age groups over 35 indicates that for some of the vergers at any rate the ties to the voting booth are beginning to break. Probably, one can be no more certain than that, for the younger vergers the voting habit will break down, while those closer to 55 will continue to enter the booth.

Mary L. is one of the vergers. She answered all the cynicism and political impotence questions in the affirmative. She is 56 years old, lives in central Pennsylvania where her husband is a bricklayer, and they grow Christmas trees on their 220 acres to make extra money. It's a family business; she and her husband and son do all the work themselves. Mary L., who is a college graduate and a Democrat, doesn't think much of politicians in general. "You get the impression from reading all that stuff in the paper . . . sometimes I don't think they are honest. In the beginning [when they first get elected] I think they do try. But it's hard bucking a stone wall. One man can't buck three men." She isn't too happy with the way things are going in America either. The taxes are going up and too many foreign goods come in free. "I don't think they should use foreign steel, when the steelworkers aren't working here." Also she is "not in favor of giving too much to poor people."

She is positive, however, about voting. "Seems as if you don't vote, it's a negative vote. You are voting for what you don't want. . . . It does make a difference to me to vote. Maybe I don't always know what I'm voting for, but I vote. . . . If you're against something you've got to vote. Otherwise you are voting for something you don't want." Mary L. also believes in planning ahead: "You do have to plan—the harder you work the more good luck you have."

Talking to Mary L. one gets the impression that her feelings of cynicism about politics and politicians and her

feelings of powerlessness are abstractions. Things in the newspaper cause her to feel this way, but they are remote feelings. In
her own life she has satisfactions and responsibilities as a
citizen. But if an event or an issue were ever to hit her
personally, the ingredients are there to create a refrainer.

James L. in Syracuse, New York, does not believe in
planning. His connection to voting seems quite tenuous. He is
49 years old, married, with five children, and he works as a
roofer, making just under $10,000 a year. He is particularly
proud of his skill in constructing slate roofs. As a verger, he too
scored 100 percent on feelings of both cynicism and political
powerlessness. He voted for Wallace in 1968, Nixon in 1972,
Carter in 1976. He thinks Carter is doing all right, but not as
well as he hoped. "I'd keep my nose out of Africa for one thing."
And he feels Carter should treat the veterans better. "If I were
on welfare I could get free glasses. But I go to the V.A. hospital
and I can't get them. On welfare they give them to you whether
you want them or not."

Then there is the problem of minorities forcing their
way into his union, affecting his ability to get work. "Why
should a minority be able to come in and get jobs ahead of me.
I know I can do twice as much work as they can." Asked if there
was anyone he would really like to see in the White House as
President he laughed and said, "No one except myself."

With such feelings, why does James L., who believes in
luck, continue to vote? "You're not going to change anything if
you don't vote." He paused and thought: "But maybe you're
not going to change anything if you do. So I don't know." But
he added after a bit that he thought he'd keep on voting
because then "at least you've got a chance" to make things
better.

Louis M. is 30 years old. He is very happy, believes in
planning ahead, has some college, and is making about $18,000
a year as a dry wall builder. He also is married and is expecting
his first child. He voted in the last four elections, is both
completely alienated and cynical with strong political views.

"My basic concern is that it's all controlled by big
business. Big business speaks and everyone jumps. No one
thinks about the little man."

He voted for Ford although he is a Democrat and
would have preferred Teddy Kennedy. He is not too happy

about Carter. "I think he smiles too much and got a knife in your back. . . . All that stuff he promises. Nothing has come about. Only thing that went up was the price of peanuts." This last particularly annoys Louis M. because he likes peanuts; he stops at a specialty store on the way home from work most nights to get them fresh roasted. He feels Carter is controlled by big business also. "He was a no name, a nothing, and some big shots were working behind the scenes." Congress, he finds as bad if not worse. "Why do we have to have so many committees and a subcommittee with a subcommittee with a subcommittee. Also I can't see where any Congressman can use $6,000 a year for writing paper. That's what they get. You're a reporter, could you use that much [paper]?"

Has he ever thought of not voting? "No, I keep on voting for change. Kennedy did the best for change. He didn't care what big business wanted. He was for the little man. . . . I'm looking at Jerry Brown. He reminds me a lot of Ford; got that spunk and gumption. . . . [The vote] is the most important tool I've got."

Louis M. is certain that his parents always vote. In fact his mother worked at the polls for ten years. For him, as for so many others, the vote has a close to magic bond that prevails over his alienation and cynicism. But how long will this magic work?

To increase the voting turnout, we need to consider both voter and refrainer, and to be concerned about the trade-offs in what we do. We have to bring refrainers to the booth and keep vergers voting, showing particular concern for the elderly vergers who have trouble getting to the polls. Certain actions advocated to increase turnout may draw some refrainers to the booth but are equally likely to drive away certain vergers. Vergers, like other voters, vote out of a feeling of duty and moral obligation, even out of an "old-fashioned" sense that voting is a privilege.

Marion C., a verger who landed in Boston from Ireland in 1920 and who now, at the age of 79, lives outside of Denver with an unmarried daughter, summed it up when she said: "I was so happy to get my citizenship papers. I went to school to get them. . . . Since I got my citizenship I always try to vote. . . . I think it is your duty. . . . As long as you vote you are supporting your country."

That's the old ethic. To sell voting like used cars, or make registration another part of junk mail affluence, both actions being advocated by well-meaning groups of people, dilutes this moral imperative of the vote.

Now that we understand who votes and who refrains we can intelligently examine some of the plans to halt the continuing increase in not voting. But first we have to face up to a question of political philosophy. Do we want large numbers of refrainers back? Are they worth the bother? We have reformed our political process so that practically anyone who wants to can vote. Are we not now better off if just those vote who really care?

4.

QUESTIONS AND SOLUTIONS

Now that we see the refrainers clearly, we can tackle the question: Do we want all these outsiders to vote? Or is democracy best served, as Thomas Jefferson and others have held, when only a small group of educated and concerned citizens go to the polls?

Herewith Senator Sam Ervin, hero of the Watergate investigation, on the subject: "I'm not going to shed any real or political or crocodile tears if people don't care enough to vote. I don't believe in making it easy for apathetic, lazy people. I'd be extremely happy if nobody in the United States voted except for the people who thought about the issues and made up their own minds and wanted to vote. No one else who votes is going to contribute anything but statistics, and I don't care that much for statistics."

Pondering Senator Ervin, an observer with a sense of history might remark that the late Senator Joseph McCarthy, of red-baiting fame, was selected in 1952 in a Wisconsin election in which 71 percent of the eligible voters turned out, whereas two years later Sam Ervin was victorious in a North Carolina election in which only 26 percent of the voters turned out. Does this make Joe McCarthy three times as good a senator as Sam Ervin?

We now question the idea of unlimited growth, once one of our most sacred beliefs. Is our belief in a constantly expanding number of voters another shibboleth whose time has passed? Consider one of the most famous expansions of the voting franchise in recent fiction.

There stands McMurphy on the floor of the ward in *One Flew Over the Cuckoo's Nest*, challenging Big Nurse Ratched on her own turf. The battle is over whether he and the other patients can watch the World Series. They agree to a vote. The first day McMurphy only gets six of the patients to stand against the nurse and vote to watch TV. By the end of the week, he gets all twenty, 100 percent of the therapy group. "There they stand, all twenty of them, raising not just for watching TV, but against Big Nurse . . . against the way she's talked and acted and beat them down for years."

But what happens?

"I count only twenty, Mr. McMurphy."

"Twenty? Well, why not? Twenty is all of us there—" His voice hangs as he realizes what she means. "Now hold on just a goddamn minute, Lady—"

"I'm afraid the vote is defeated. There are forty patients on the ward, Mr. McMurphy. Forty patients and only twenty voted! . . ."

Nurse Ratched has dramatically doubled the franchise to include all those in the beds too disturbed to either hear or move. This sudden expansion of the right to vote hardly appears as a democratic triumph.

And such disturbing moments do not just occur in fiction. After the Reichstag fire Adolf Hitler expanded the numbers of those voting from 75.6 percent in 1928 to 88.8 percent in 1933. And by grabbing the allegiance of the previous nonvoters he was able to place himself firmly in power.

Philosophers and social scientists as disparate as John Stuart Mill, John Locke, Aristotle, Plato, Thomas Jefferson, and Joseph Schumpeter have thought that small- to medium-sized turnouts might be best for democratic government. Such a view may be out of fashion today, but no worthy study of nonvoting, its causes, effects, and cures, can lightly dismiss the conclusions of such men.

The writings of John Stuart Mill against slavery and in support of the North during the Civil War still rank among the great defenses of liberty, yet Mill was disturbed by the weaknesses of democracy caused by the right of everyone to vote. He finally devised a system of weighted ballots where each vote counted more as a person's education increased. Those who had graduated from college were to have seven times as many votes as those just able to read and write.

John Locke, one of our intellectual fathers, was continually qualifying his ideas of equality and democracy. "Though I have said that all men by nature are equal, I cannot be supposed to understand all sorts of equality. Age or virtue may give men a just precedence. Excellence of parts and merit may place others above the common level. Birth may subject some, and alliance or benefits others, to pay an observance to those whom nature, gratitude, or other respects may have made it due."

Aristotle felt that many men were slaves by nature and did not want freedom. He would entrust the right to vote only to the middle class and aristocrats, excluding tradesmen and craftsmen, because he felt the upper classes alone had the background and training to maintain democracy. Plato, who felt much the same way, gave the vote to tradesmen and craftsmen but excluded poets, painters, and flute players as too frivolous to govern themselves. Thomas Jefferson wished, after the country had been established a number of years, to restrict the vote to high school graduates, and of course he excluded women and slaves.

A more modern argument in favor of restricted turnouts has been excellently put by Joseph Schumpeter in *Capitalism, Socialism, and Democracy*. Schumpeter believed: "Democracy is a political method, that is to say, a certain type of institutional arrangement for arriving at political-legislative and administrative decisions and hence incapable of being an end in itself. . . . Democracy is a system in which elites compete for limited political goals. The people do not really govern themselves any more, if in fact they ever did. Most people act irrationally when they are faced with the complex political choices which modern society presents."

For Schumpeter democracy had nothing to do with freedom of speech, or conscience, or equality, or justice, all of which, he argued, might be better obtained under some other system. "In the most famous of all trials," he noted, "Pilate was, from the standpoint of the Jews, certainly the representative of autocracy. Yet he tried to protect freedom. And he yielded to democracy."

Schumpeter was writing in a world atmosphere made chaotic by the revolutions of Hitler, Stalin, and to some extent Freud. His view of political man was a lot closer to that of Hieronymus Bosch or Pieter Breughel than of Plato or Locke. "The typical citizen drops down to a lower level of mental performance as soon as he enters the political field. He argues and analyzes in a way which he would readily recognize as infantile within the sphere of his real interests. He becomes a primitive again. His thinking becomes associative and affective. . . . If for once he does emerge from his usual vagueness and does display the definite will postulated by the classical doctrine of democracy, he is as likely as not to become still more unintelligent and irresponsible than he usually is. At certain junctures, this may prove fatal to his nation."

Schumpeter and other modern "realists" deny the idea of any common good that can be discerned by the average citizen. This idea they feel is an eighteenth century fallacy, a hand-me-down from medieval Christian thought that postulated God's purpose in the world. Since there is no one just goal for the voters to discern, large turnouts simply distort the competition for power among various elites.*

A current refinement to this argument holds that though a large turnout is a desirable goal, just at the present things are so complicated that small turnouts and elite decisions are to be preferred. This argument is often advanced about the "developing countries" or the so-called "third world." People in these countries, so the argument runs, are held to have such limited experience of democracy and be so undereducated that the governance of these areas is best left to the few with education and experience.

One also hears the same argument applied to today's America. Right now the traditional values that have held society and democracy together have broken down. The very life of the nation is up for grabs. In such an explosive, lawless, ungoverned

---

*The data contain a powerful argument against this thesis. Namely, that many refrainers are better educated and politically aware than some of the voters.

moment, small turnouts are a blessing. They remove from the decision process those most likely to make the wrong decisions.

Professor Burnham P. Beckwith carries the argument for small turnouts to its "logical" conclusion. For him the ideal democracy is a government run by social scientists who are elected only by other social scientists. "And they will rule for the benefit of society as a whole, not for the benefit of the intellectual and professional class." How will they do this? Because through the techniques of social science they can perceive the common good. Rousseau's Roi Philosophe wears a mortarboard and carries a pocket computer.

Some few argue that not voting is as much a right as voting. They fear that the effort to increase the turnout will lead to legislation such as that in Australia, where people are fined for refraining. Small turnouts they see as a defense against an odious 1984 type of society where everything not prohibited is obligatory. To force, even forcefully to urge people to vote is another erosion of freedom, a whittling away of a basic American right, the right not to vote.

In addition to these arguments in favor of low turnouts, politics rears its fascinating head. Republicans, whose voters are fewer, older, wealthier, better educated, and more likely to vote, find low turnouts to their benefit. It used to be said that the Republican formula for carrying Michigan was "To pray like hell election day for rain in Detroit." Democrats, whom our refrainers favor three to one, favor the high turnouts that will benefit them.*

History and this study of refrainers indicate that in the short term, say one election, the Democrats will certainly benefit from an enlarged turnout. But which Democrats? That cannot be predicted. It depends on which refrainers start for the booth first. Democratic refrainers interviewed were as likely to be for George Wallace as for George McGovern. As for the long-term effects of increased turnouts on the makeup of our political parties, these too are indiscernible, at least by us. There are a great many predictions being floated, but the data support none of them.

Turning to the philosophical supporters of large turnouts, they take the same observation, that diminished turnouts

---

*But see pages 58–59. Those refrainers turned into Republicans in the Eisenhower years.

favor government by elites and use this as an argument *against* small turnouts. With ever decreasing numbers of people voting in America they see an ascendency of interest group politics. They feel this fragments America and separates people from their government. The answer to the dangers of government by elites is to have more people voting. Basically democracy rests on the will of the people and large turnouts, while not always perfect, form the most secure base for democratic judgment.

In our own prosaic time, when eloquence in political argument is unusual, Isaiah Berlin has brilliantly upheld the benefits of large turnouts. He has been particularly critical of the view that large turnouts may be a fine goal but at present things are so complicated that restricted turnouts are necessary while the elites decide. He argues that there would always occur some new crisis requiring that cool heads and stout hearts keep power from the masses a while longer.

"Participation in self-government," Berlin wrote, "is, like justice, a basic human requirement, and end in itself."

In his essay, "Two Concepts of Liberty," Berlin developed the argument that to function, a government must either make people feel a part of itself or coerce them into performing. Voting makes people feel a part of the government. The more people who vote, the more people who feel a part of the government, the less coercion is necessary. The data support this particular argument. Refrainers were substantially more likely to show signs of political impotence than even those voters who had voted for a defeated political party.

The act of voting appears to force a person to grow up politically, to learn certain truths about himself. Twenty-eight percent of the refrainers did not know if they were moderate, conservative, or liberal. Even among the vergers only 18 percent lacked such insights into themselves, while only 14 percent of the voters as a whole were unable to decide. To vote, like being hanged, appears wonderfully to concentrate the mind.

But here a word of warning. Voters become refrainers for a variety of reasons. An important reason is voting, winning, and then not getting what you want. Congressmen are elected who are against busing; busing goes on. A president is elected to stop the war; the war goes on. A mayor is elected to reduce bureaucracy and crime; both increase. More and more citizens see examples of the elites making decisions that are against the will of the majority. And the majority need no poll to tell them this. Or the decisions are made in places the voters can't reach or influence, such as the courts or the bureaucracy. All this leads to growing feelings of impotence.

The beneficial effect of voting on the voters is continually stressed by philosophers who favor increased turnouts. John Stuart Mill was eloquent on the subject, even though he wanted to weight the ballot in favor of the educated. He found voting "a great influence acting on the human mind. . . . Among the foremost benefits of free government is that education of the intelligence and of the sentiments which is carried down to the lowest ranks of the people when they are called to take part in acts which directly affect the great interests of the country."

Speaking for today, Isaiah Berlin agrees: "All paternalist governments, however benevolent, cautious, disinterested, and rational, have tended, in the end, to treat the majority of men as minors, or as being too often incurably foolish or irresponsible; or else as maturing so slowly as not to justify their liberation at any clearly foreseeable date (which, in practice, means at no definite time at all). This is a policy which degrades men. . . ."

In recent American history the ability of elites to distort the political process when turnouts are small is most evident in the Presidential primaries. So few people vote that the political activists, whether on the right or the left, can greatly influence the process. The Goldwater victory in the 1964 Republican primaries and the McGovern victory in the 1972 Democratic primaries are examples of the political system's being distorted by activists functioning brilliantly in a low turnout environment.

When voting is low those in power become more apt to pay attention to those who grab their ears by methods other than voting. Such methods include campaign contributions, threats to withhold or grant the support of organized groups, all forms of lobbying, media manipulation, favors, and sympathetic reporting. Pollsters and reporters also achieve inordinate influence in situations of low turnout. Since the public does not bother to record its preference by voting, the politician relies heavily on the pollster or the reporter to tell him "what is out there." In this process, the wishes of the voters are often frustrated, their feelings of political impotence increase, and therefore refraining rises. Small turnouts are self-reflexive. They lead to smaller turnouts.

More recently—and most dramatically in events such as the McGovern campaign, the protests against the Vietnam War, and lobbying efforts of consumer groups like Ralph Nader's—the politically active have bypassed the voter and have gone directly to the media, mostly television, to influence politicians. Indeed, certain groups may even risk a negative influence on the voter in their efforts to "bring media pressure" on political leaders. Airplane hijackings by the PLO are an example of media pressure on elites that alienates voters.

From the results of our survey it appears this emphasis on television by political activists is an important cause of refraining—not television itself, but the way it has been exploited. Formerly those people who cared deeply about an issue, the high-status 5 percent of Americans who form the activists in any political situation, tried to get their ideas adopted by working on the voters to change their minds. Then the voters voted differently and the politicians responded. The abolition of slavery and the issue of free trade versus protection were classic battles fought in this manner. In this process the voters as they were appealed to by both sides felt rightly that they were important. Voting was important, and voters had status. Refrainers formed a small percentage of the electorate.

But the activists in bypassing the voter and changing the elite-to-media-to-voter-to-politician relationship to the shorter form of elite-to-media-to-politician help increase feelings of voter powerlessness. Such an increase leads to further refraining. Voters feel rightly that they are being left out of the system and join the 22 percent of refrainers who feel extreme political impotence, along with the 21 percent of voters whose feelings categorized them as vergers. At the same time, the political elite, finding it easier to use television to pressure politicians than to take the slower route of persuading voters, tended themselves to become contemptuous of the democratic process. So bit by bit in hidden ways low turnouts breed lower turnouts.

So where does this book stand in this argument? Are large turnouts important? Should refrainers be encouraged and aided to become voters? The answer is yes. We recognize many of the arguments against large turnouts as valid. To ignore what Hitler accomplished through broadening the franchise or to believe that Italy, where 93 percent of the people vote, is better governed than America, where 54 percent of the people vote, is to turn one's back on both news and history. But in this media-oriented, high-pressure age the arguments against low turnouts are equally valid.

America's present problem is not a violently split society where everyone is voting. It is an apathetic, cross-pressured society with strong feelings of political impotence, where more and more people find their lives out of control, believe in luck, and refrain from voting. These growing numbers of refrainers hang over the democratic process like a bomb, ready to explode and change the course of our history as they have twice in our past. For us, now, an increase in voting is a sign of political health.

It should be emphasized once again that voters change their political beliefs and their political parties slowly, if at all; but refrainers change their political beliefs and parties with lightning-like rapidity. Both times in our history when there have been large numbers of refrainers, sudden radical shifts of power have occurred. As long as the present gigantic mass of refrainers sits outside our political system, neither we nor our allies can be certain of even the normally uncertain future. This is why creating voters, bringing the refrainers to the booth, is important. An increasing number of voters would indicate an increasingly stable American society with common goals. Of course there are circumstances where the rush of refrainers to the polls would indicate extreme political turmoil; for example, if large numbers of the positive apathetics suddenly felt their life styles threatened and started to vote. That is why it is preferable to start increasing the number of voters now, before any such event.

Further, democracy is at once both a system of government that can be analyzed and an ideal that is the subject of emotional belief. Political man needs both bread and the word: socioeconomics and faith. By the act of voting we accept those traditions of service, common good, and public interest that historically were given by God to guide monarch or aristocracy. To vote is both a political act to get something and a moral act to accept responsibility for the future. In this age where responsibility is suspect, no wonder so few reach the booth. To vote is to accept choice. To choose is to be alive.

Now having said we believe it important to increase turnouts, to refill the booth, we must deal with a popular myth about large turnouts that appears emphatically untrue.

This myth is that large turnouts produce good government, that government gets better as voting increases. Turnout and the quality of government have little to do with each other. An increase in voting won't make our government any better; an increase in refraining, which is more probable, won't make it any worse. Is Italy, where 93 percent of the electorate vote, better governed than Sweden, where 88 percent vote? And are both better governed than America, where 54 percent vote, and Great Britain, where 72 percent vote? Is Minnesota with 72 percent voting better run than Alaska with 53 percent voting? Are William Henry Harrison, Zachary Taylor, and Franklin Pierce, our only three Presidents elected with over 80 percent of the eligibles voting, our three greatest Presidents? To ask these questions is to know the answer. Between turnout size and government excellence exists zero correlation.

Having decided—at least in theory—that it is beneficial to increase turnout size: How will the refrainers be brought into the system? And equally important, how will those voters who are on the verge of not voting, 21 percent of all of the voters, be kept in the booth?

We have seen our refrainers to be complex people, different from each other, much like voters yet separated from them by feelings of powerlessness, lack of control, apathy. No magic programs, pollster-determined buzz-words, political slogans, or partisan rhetoric will bring these refrainers to the polls as a group. But this does not mean that some combination of issue and candidate will not make voters out of many in the immediate future. Unfortunately, the data have revealed no amazing solutions or sweeping answers for the problem of refraining. Nor can we manufacture a bionic candidate to ease our woes.

To focus as the country does now, largely on the bypassed refrainer, 13 percent of the refrainers, is to make the same mistake we did in the Sixties when we tried to save the central cities of America. It was thought then that the first priority should be transforming the worst parts, the central

slums. This was found to consume billions, tear apart neighborhoods, and leave cities the same as before if not worse. Now
we attack first those neighborhoods that are still viable. Our
data indicate that the bypassed refrainers are among the least
likely to return to the booth.

Refraining today in America is rising fastest among the
educated and the relatively affluent. These are the groups—the
positive apathetics, the cross-pressured, and the physically
disenfranchised—that should be reached first. The bypassed
and the naysayers come later. The politically impotent will
most probably move back into the system on their own,
somewhere in the middle period.

The question is one of time, money, and human
energy. We have only finite resources to devote to this problem,
and they should be used where they can do the most good.
Some will feel this approach is backwards, holding it society's
duty to assist the undereducated and underprivileged to the
booth first. That's another argument, another book. This one is
about political refraining, repopulating the voting booth.

What then is the best method to bring the refrainers to
the booth? Before turning to specific items of reform, the
overall sweep of what we have discovered should be reempha-
sized. Twelve percent refrained because they were physically
disenfranchised. Six percent could not vote or register for
reasons of health; technical changes will help both these
groups. Thirteen percent are bypassed refrainers who felt they
lacked both knowledge and motivation to vote; massive information campaigns and voting aid could reach them, but they
are, as a group, least likely to vote. The rest of the sample, about
70 percent, did not vote because they felt the act meaningless or
they lacked a reason to go to the polls.

The vast majority of the refrainers will return to the
polls for political reasons. It's not a surprising truth when you
think about it—though one can see why politicians prefer to
believe that vast numbers of people who want to vote are being
excluded from the polls, rather than face the music that they
themselves are behaving in such a way that 60 percent of the
refrainers feel alienated from them and 35 percent, the positive
apathetics, find them irrelevant. To be blunt: it is their disgust
with politicians, not needed "reforms," that are keeping the
refrainers from the polls.

Good candidates and believable issues the candidate can make his or her own will make refrainers vote. When asked what would bring them back to the booth, the refrainers answered over and over: "Better candidates," "Someone who tells the truth," "A man you can trust." Or as Pease D., the security guard in York, Pennsylvania, put it: "If I saw a good man I'd vote for him. But after Watergate how do you know?"

There is no art that can tell a candidate what is the magic issue that will bring refrainers into the booth voting for him or her. What combination of beliefs, needs, and fears will emerge to cause the apathetic to become interested, the "luckers" to believe their vote counts, and the impotent to feel the urge to use their latent political power. That the refrainers are liable to appear as voters, suddenly in large numbers, grouped behind some candidate is indicated by our history. But at this writing, at least to this somewhat experienced eye, the outline of the new political formations are no more in evidence than the location of Maitland's Guards behind their embankment at Waterloo.

One further aspect of the survey that was qualitative rather than quantitative should be emphasized again. Both voters and refrainers regarded voting as a moral obligation. Voters were not just voting to get something; they were voting because they felt it the right thing to do. This is the force particularly important in holding in the booth the 21 percent of voters who had all the characteristics of refrainers. This is the force that makes refrainers, particularly college-educated, upper-income refrainers, report they voted when they refrained.

"We feel badly we weren't registered," said Betty Ann D., who works in a sewing machine factory in central Pennsylvania and sells Tupperware on the side. "We will vote in the next election."

"I just got a feeling' that come the next election, I will vote. The way the world's going these days people ought to," explained Peggy L. in rural West Virginia, who at 56 has yet to vote. She remembers clearly that her father and mother always voted.

Georgia Q., in Toledo, watched the debates, usually votes in local elections, cared who won, and yet still refrained. She told us: "I have to state that I feel it is important to vote.

And sometimes I feel that I haven't fulfilled myself as a citizen. And I did feel guilty after I didn't vote."

Bonaparte E., an Air Force paramedic who had just retired and moved to the outskirts of Houston, put it this way: "As far as voting is concerned I feel it a privilege that you have to voice your opinions on who will run the country."

Over and over the refrainers repeated this theme. Any action that reinforces the moral obligations of the vote will both bring refrainers to the polls and hold the vergers in the booth.

This is why proposals "to sell voting like soap," on the assumption that the vast majority of the refrainers are Boobus Americanus, are so pernicious. By treating voting as a commodity, they cheapen its value, lower its status, and destroy its symbolic power. A bunch of talking voting booths, or gyrating topless dancers with "vote" tatooed on their breasts is not going to increase the turnout, though cosmetic politicians and newspapers and TV networks, who benefit from the increased advertising, claim that it will. Such tactics, by debasing the moral coinage of the vote, make refraining among certain groups more likely.

Although better candidates and relevant issues will be the major cause of increased turnouts, nevertheless, since many of the factors leading to refraining are sociological and psychological, other basic changes in the refrainers' lives can help them become voters. For example, we have noted the high percentage of women among the bypassed refrainers, 67 percent. These women all suffer from damaged feelings of self-worth.

"I haven't had the opportunity to take up politics. I don't have too much education," said Peggy L., 56 years old, who lives with her husband in rural West Virginia. "It's a small town, but a clean town."

Mrs. Mabel D. of Corpus Christi, who is 60 years old and has never voted, put it even more strongly: "My daddy didn't believe women should vote. It was for the men."

For women such as these many of the activities associated with women's liberation will be of value in bringing them to the polls. Since refraining is such a decisive function of psychic impotence, anything that produces a greater feeling of competence among these women and control over their lives is certain to increase the numbers of them voting. One can find other areas where activities outside the conventional structure of politics will help decrease refraining.

For example the critical divide between refrainers and voters was whether they believed in planning or luck. Any trends in the country that increase people's feelings of personal control will bring them to the polls. If employment is high, job satisfactions increase, the environment improves, war ceases to be so grimly close, more people stay married, children conform to the wishes of their elders, crime decreases, any one of these happenings will increase the numbers of those who believe in planning and will start to refill the booth.

Here the positive apathetics distort the picture. If things go decisively better, in addition to more people voting, more people will join the ranks of the positive apathetics. And if things get decisively worse, some of the positive apathetics will be jolted into voting. But in the main, an increase in life satisfactions will increase voting.

Some specific suggestions to halt refraining follow, and also some criticisms of current proposals. To some these suggestions may seem puny beside the number of refrainers. This is deliberate. Many of the solutions being suggested today are based on false premises of who the refrainers are. Their costs are great, their possible rewards small. The data indicate—and other surveys tend to support this—that the most that can be hoped for by reform of registration and voting is a temporary increase in voters of less than 10 percent—hardly an improvement worth prodigious money and labor, particularly when turnout has no effect on how well or badly we are governed. We have tried to base our solutions on the data and keep them simple.

In the move to increase the voting turnout it seems to us important to leave a great deal of latitude to the states. They provide fifty different test areas where various political and social solutions can be tried out. Let the Federal government set the standards and leave the states to impose their solutions and see which ones work best. And as they do so, beware of those misleading statistics from Wisconsin and Minnesota, those two states with relaxed registration rules and high turnouts; but also with rising rates of refraining.

Take the complex question of how the length and size of the ballot affect voting. This is an area where no one has final answers. Some believe long ballots draw citizens to the polls because of the interest in special issues, local elections, citizen referenda, bond issues, and other such items of intimate concern to voters. Others, equally committed, believe the lengthy ballot puts people off, trivializes the whole process by making the voters choose among hordes of people none of whom they know, for minor offices. Will more people really turn out to vote for mayor, police chief, sanitation inspector, and road supervisor, they ask, than just for mayor—particularly when they realize that to vote for so many removes the authority of the mayor to fire the police chief? Until there are convincing answers to such questions the Federal government should not impose a given ballot length on all states.

As with ballot length, so with other recommendations to increase turnout. Even solutions which our data indicated would work, such as a greater use of the absentee ballot, we believe should be left to the states to implement. Political traditions are different in New York, Georgia, North Dakota, and Alaska. To create costly Federal machinery to impose uniformity is the wrong approach. Besides, the Federal government is a poor watchdog over itself. Witness the Justice Department's failure to police crimes committed by other Federal agencies. To leave the action to the states and to give the Federal government a watchdog function over them seems the most efficient system, and the system most likely to produce, somewhere in its fifty parts, imaginative solutions.

The first part of the voting process that involves the citizen is the need to register. Here begins the first possibility of reform. Twelve percent of the sample cited reasons of physical disenfranchisement for not voting. Another 6 percent cited reasons of health. For some of this 18 percent changes in registration procedures will make a difference. Also some of the positive apathetic and a few of the cross-pressured might just vote if registration were made easier. And many of the vergers would be more inclined to remain in the booth.

Of that 12 percent of the refrainers who cited physical disenfranchisement as a reason for not voting, two-thirds gave as their reason either a recent move (the most common cause) or the fact that they were out of town during registration or they made up their mind too late. All of these, and some who gave miscellaneous answers, would be helped by postal card

registration, one of the basic proposals of voting reform, pro-
vided that the postal card registration be coupled with a decrease
in the length of time required for residence in certain states!

We are a mobile people and should acknowledge this
fact. Several states still have residency requirements of one year
before a person can vote, the specious argument being that it
takes this long for new arrivals to inform themselves about local
issues.

A reasonable compromise would seem to be that all
states should press toward a residency requirement of about 30
days. But again the exact length of time should be left to the
states. One of our recommendations involving voting, which
will be discussed later, looks to a far more frequent use of the
absentee ballot. By permitting people to vote from their old
neighborhood, the absentee ballot cuts down on the numbers
of those disenfranchised by lengthy residence requirements.

There is also a political reason why a shorter residency
requirement and absentee ballots are important. As has been
noted, most of the proposals to increase turnout favor Democrats. But among the recently moved and those out of town on
election day, and those who physically could not get to the
polls, the percentage of Republicans, conservative Democrats, and Independents is much higher than among refrainers
as a whole. Republicans charge, somewhat justly, that some
Democrats don't really want large turnouts, they just want more
Democrats voting. Shortening the residency requirements and
easing the absentee ballot procedures would increase the
number of Republicans and Independents voting. This makes
it a good area for political trade-offs.

Postal card registration as a term encompasses two
largely different programs, only one of which appears to be
beneficial. The key question is how the postal card gets into the
hands of the voter so that he or she can mail it back. In the
proposal favored by the postal union, the one that will cost
millions and do little, the post office mails the registration cards
to every potential voter in the country. There are a great many
objections to this proposal that have nothing to do with politics
or voting: the expense, the number of extra people the postal
service would have to hire and train, the possibilities of fraud,
what would happen to the rest of the mail—so unevenly
processed at present—while the massive mailing went out. But

beyond these substantial objections are others that bear on the efficacy of such a system. Its proponents have designed it to reach the bypassed refrainers without any idea who these people are. The stereotyped nonvoter problem again. Our survey finds that the bypassed refrainers would be the last to respond to such a mailing. Furthermore, it would not help the cross-pressured or reach the naysayer or politically impotent. Some of the positive apathetics, particularly the younger refrainers in this category, might be reached, but that's a small gain for such a massive effort.

Under this proposal an estimated 150 million forms as a minimum will have to be mailed. The Federal Elections Commission estimates the fees just for starting up the program would run over $100 million. After that they want an open-ended authorization to continue. Is this the best place to put so great a portion of our national energy, when certainly no more than 4 or 5 percent of the refrainers will be affected? Further, contact with a political party and party identification are important ingredients in voting. People who vote are more than twice as apt to have been contacted by a political party as people who don't vote. If there is unanimous agreement about any one trend in America today it is that party politics in America is declining and that this is harmful to the polity. A move that further removes the party from the registration process is apt to push a number of vergers into being refrainers. Democrats might note here that the majority of vergers belong to their party.

How then should the postal cards be gotten into the hands of potential voters? The answer is, by practically all means possible other than the post office, but preferably by some form of personal contact. Let the unions give them out, the Boy Scouts, The League of Women Voters, Common Cause, business organizations, churches, city hall. Above all let the political parties give them out. The purpose is to get as many people to vote as possible, while paying the proper attention to the possibility of fraud. Leave the distribution of the cards to people whose self-interest it is to register and bring to the polls the maximum number of people. If party members could carry registration cards with them on their canvasses for citizens to fill out and mail, registration would be increased and the role of the party strengthened. In addition, face-to-face contact with someone interested in politics not only might make it easier for refrainers to reach the polls but might reinforce their desire to do so.

Under this proposed system, the cards would be mailed back to the local board of elections, who would check them for fraud and compile public lists of voters. It is important that postal card registration end long enough before election day for these public lists to be checked by the political parties, the press, and any watchdog groups of concerned citizens. This public check of open voting lists is the best guarantee there is against fraud. The scrutiny of those who stand to lose if deceit is practiced will keep election officials on their marks.

How long before election day should the voting lists be closed? When should registration end? The question is a difficult and serious one. Some believe registration should end at least a month before election day. Others would permit the voter to register on the day of election itself merely by showing a driver's license or some other form of identification. The problem is one of both bureaucratic efficiency and election fraud.

Neither political party is entirely forthright in dealing with questions of political fraud on voting. The Republicans, fearful of large turnouts and wanting to limit voting to the more educated and affluent who make up their minds early, maneuver to block necessary registration reforms behind a smoke screen of a concern for honest voting. The Democrats, who realize that large turnouts favor their party and that many of their voters make up their minds late, push for totally open registration as if fraud did not exist. From campaigning on Watergate, they conveniently overlook Watergate. They forget the words of one of democracy's founders, Pericles of Athens, who wrote: "Of Gods we believe and of men we know, that whatever they can do they will." Closer to home they overlook large parts of American history.

And the danger is not just the possibility of fraud. There is also bureaucratic fumble and bumble, duller to write about but far more prevalent. Already Minnesota reports that in the general election of 1976 there were 13,053 faulty registrations, 47.8 percent of the total number of election-day registrations. Suppose we have another close election, as we had in 1960 and 1976, and in two or three states voting irregularities are alleged:

people not being able to vote because of long lines, voters voting in the wrong precinct, and allegations of fraud. Suppose all this is proved to be merely bureaucratic ineptitude. With same-day registration it would take a minimum of a week after the election to check out these allegations. Do we want to turn on our television sets for a whole week and hear the cheery newscaster tell us: "We don't really know who is President yet, folks. They're still checking out that mess in Louisiana and Minnesota"?

Probably registration by mail should require the cards to be postmarked thirty days before election day; and in-person registration should end the Friday before election. But again, this will have to vary from state to state. Election officials, reporters, politicians, and citizen groups must have time to check the published rolls and the names of the enrollees must be distributed to the polling places. Most surveys show that by the week before election the vast majority of the initially undecideds who are likely to vote have made up their minds. The data and our interviews tend to support this conclusion. Practically all refrainers who cite registration difficulties or last-moment doubts will be served by closing the last processes of registration the week before election day.

After registration comes V-day itself: the day one votes or refrains. Here two proposals have merit. Both aim at holding the vergers as voters while making it easier for several large classes of refrainers to enter the booth. To be fully effective they should be enacted together.

The first proposal is to make the day on which we vote a holiday, in both presidential and congressional election years. As has been stressed people regard voting as a moral obligation, a very special moment in their lives. All but the naysayers express guilt about not voting, and undoubtedly some of them justify themselves so loudly to drown their doubts. Making election day a holiday reinforces the vote's importance, just as the holiday on Sunday for years reinforced the importance of the Sabbath. The day on which we vote is the day on which our democracy is reborn. We should honor our embattled political religion with a holiday. We owe ourselves a little something.

Those who gave as their reasons for not voting "out of town" or "had to work," about 5 percent of our sample, will, of course benefit directly from a holiday. But more important, the vote will be made more attractive for much larger classes of refrainers: the positive apathetics, the cross-pressured, and the politically impotent. Anything that makes the vote more important will help break their refraining habits, and also help hold the vergers in the booth. Furthermore, today's children are tomorrow's voters or refrainers. Children like holidays, particularly holidays that fall during the time they are in school. A holiday dedicated to voting will have a lasting impact on their lives.

As this proposal has been tried out on people, it has met some serious opposition from economists who claim that there is too much hidden cost, that in these perilous times we cannot afford the GNP loss that a holiday would cause. Somehow we cannot take these caveats of the gloomy science seriously. All our life is not yet spent in playing holiday. We can enjoy a day off every two years to vote, particularly when the result will be a long-term increase in voting turnout.

The second proposal is that absentee ballots be made far more easily and readily available than now. This proposal strikes directly at the largest portion of refrainers, the 35 percent who are positive apathetics. It also strikes directly at those numerous refrainers whose characteristics were most like those of the voters, the elderly in ill health as well as the other physically disenfranchised, such as the recently moved and the "out of town" on election day. Further, by making voting easier for everyone, it encourages the vergers, 22 percent of the voters, to stay in the system.

As long as the refrainers were viewed as Boobus Americanus such a proposal made no sense. Absentee ballots wouldn't reach the then envisioned "nonvoter." But for the majority of refrainers as they actually exist, absentee ballots make total sense. It's a proposal that aids the groups most likely to start voting.

Again there is an important political trade-off here. The positive apathetics, the "healths," and the "out of towns" are, like all refrainers, more Democratic than Republican. (But remember that refrainers tend to be Republican in years Republicans win and Democratic in years Democrats win. They don't have as much political commitment as voters. That's part of what makes them so volatile and dangerous.) However, these groups of refrainers contain the greatest number of Republicans and Independents. Republicans and moderate to conservative Democrats might well be induced to support other important reforms, like postal card registration, in return for liberal Democratic support of easier to obtain absentee ballots—and vice versa. The people absentee ballots will help already shop by mail, use credit card numbers. They can vote by mail using registration card numbers. When you think about it, going to the voting booth in this modern electronic world is a pretty obsolescent procedure.

Specifically, everyone on social security because of age, or anyone receiving a disability pension, should automatically receive an absentee ballot. Their address and existence have been investigated for them to receive their benefit check. For other voters a written request received up to six weeks before election day, or a visit to the election office up to the week before election should be sufficient. There are problems here, undoubtedly, in safeguarding against fraud. We are in the gray world of trade-offs. But the potential gain is great with easier absentee ballots because we are reaching out to both the largest group of refrainers and those most likely to vote.

The positive apathetics can have their holiday with their children, or continue their work, or go to the lake or out camping, and vote too. The present overreporters can mail in their ballot and enjoy their holiday without guilt. Those in ill health, watching the election on TV, particularly the housebound senior citizens, will know the country still cares about them. The easier absentee ballot will do more to increase the numbers of those voting than any proposal now under serious consideration.

This book came about because the writer and the pollster believed not voting is the dominant fact in American politics. We felt that refraining was on the rise in part because no one understood who the refrainers were. We couldn't believe that 65 million Americans were the know-nothings they were so often thought to be or that large groups were still being kept from the polls against their will as they had been until the 1960's.

Our study uncovered a great deal about refrainers that had been unknown or only dimly perceived. We saw that refrainers did not vote because of their attitudes towards life and politics, rather than because of education, economics, or legal or physical restraints. For example, there was the amazing difference between refrainers and voters over whether they planned ahead or believed in luck. We looked at each other with a wild surmise when that turned up. We found that refrainers differed markedly from each other in their reasons for not voting, and that they could be divided into major categories because of those reasons: The positive apathetics, the bypassed, the politically impotent, the physically disenfranchised, the naysayers, and the cross-pressured.

This better understanding of the refrainers, and of the vergers, the voters most like refrainers, helps explain other aspects of the American political landscape: George Wallace's popularity, the rise of the Independents, support and opposition in the Vietnam War, the strength of the two parties, Carter's victory. It also helps predict what actions will increase voting and what actions won't.

However knowing more about the refrainers should not lessen our anxiety over their enlarging numbers or our concern over the sudden shifts they could force on America. As there is a critical mass of nuclear material necessary to trigger an atomic explosion so there appears to be a critical percentage of nonvoters necessary to produce rapid political change. Historically that percentage has been close to the 50 percent we now approach. They sit out there, that great mass of refrainers, disconnected from the process of democracy, but able at any moment to dominate our future. Our future is their future. To start them back now as voters is important. Not because our country will necessarily be governed better if they return, but because their growing presence menaces any government.

NOTES

1. WHO DOES NOT VOTE: MYTH AND FACT

(p. 16, l. 3)   Since there are a variety of sources for election turn-
                  out figures, the numbers can vary. We have decided
                  to use the following sources:
                  For national and state turnouts in the presidential
                  election of 1976, *Congressional Quarterly Weekly Report*,
                  December 18, 1976, p. 3333.
                  For national and state turnouts in 1960–1974, U.S.
                  Bureau of the Census, *Statistical Abstract of the United
                  States: 1975* (96th edition). Washington, D.C., 1975,
                  p. 451.
                  For national turnout in presidential elections in
                  1928–1956, Mackie and Rose, p. 427.
                  For election figures before 1928, individual sources
                  as cited.

(p. 17, l. 2)   The Truman-Dewey election of 1948, where only
                  51.1 percent of the electorate turned out, the lowest
                  between 1928 and 1976, was a peculiar dip, pro-
                  duced by short-term political circumstances.

(p. 17, l. 16)   Hofstadter et al., p. 264.

(p. 17, l. 25)   Nie, Verba, and Petrocik, p. 87.

(p. 18, l. 23)   U.S. Government, Department of Commerce, Bu-
                  reau of the Census, *Voting and Registration in the Elec-
                  tion of 1972*.

(p. 18, l. 33)   Groupings of the states into the major geographical
                      regions roughly parallel those of the U.S. Bureau of
                      the Census.
(p. 18, l. 38)   See Appendix B, Table 2.
(p. 19, l. 7)   Flanigan and Zingale, p. 15, Figure 1.1, Estimated
                      Turnout in Presidential Elections in the South and
                      Non-South, 1860–1972.
(p. 19, l. 10)   See note for p. 10.
(p. 19, Fn.)   U.S. Bureau of the Census, *Voter Participation in
                      November 1976* (Advance Report), p. 1.
(p. 20, l. 19)   *Ibid.,* p. 3.
(p. 20, Fn.)   U.S. Bureau of the Census, *Voter Participation in
                      November 1976,* p. 3.
(p. 20, l. 31)   Nie, Verba, and Petrocik, p. 278, data from the
                      Survey Research Center, University of Michigan.
                      The SRC national surveys of the American voter,
                      begun in 1952, provide the definitive body of elec-
                      tion data which is the basic reference for all other
                      work on voting behavior in United States national
                      elections.
(p. 21, l. 17)   Peter D. Hart, "Nonvoter Study 1976," Committee
                      for the Study of the American Electorate.
(p. 22, l. 34)   Nie, Verba, and Petrocik, p. 276.
(p. 25, l. 6)   Smolka, Preface.
(p. 25, l. 22)   *Newsweek,* January 24, 1977.
(p. 26, l. 41)   Campbell et al., p. 111.
(p. 27, l. 27)   Clausen, "Response Validity: Vote Report," 1967
                      manuscript, p. 19. Article later published in *Public
                      Opinion Quarterly.*
(p. 28, l. 21)   *Newsday* poll conducted in August 1976 among 648
                      Nassau and Suffolk residents.
(p. 28, l. 31)   *Newsday: LI,* February 22, 1976, p. 10.
(p. 30, l. 5)   *The Washington Post,* October 31, 1976.
(p. 34, l. 22)   See Appendix B, Table 1.
(p. 35, l. 13)   See Appendix B, Table 3.
(p. 35, l. 33)   Nie, Verba, and Petrocik, pp. 278–79.
(p. 36, l. 7)   See Appendix B, Table 1.
(p. 38, l. 17)   Campbell et al., p. 106.
(p. 39, l. 38)   See Appendix A.

2. REFRAINING: FROM PLYMOUTH ROCK THROUGH THE NEW DEAL

(p. 45, l. 13)   *Select Documents of English Constitutional History,* ed.
                      George Burton Adams and H. Morse Stephens
                      (New York: The Macmillan Company, 1921), p.
                      190, quoted in Chute, p. 16.
(p. 47, l. 4)   *The Federal and State Constitutions, Colonial Charters, and*

Other Organic Laws of the States, Territories, and Colonies Now or Heretofore Forming the United States of America, 7 vols., ed. Francis Newton Thorpe, (Washington: Government Printing Office, 1909), V, 2772, quoted in Chute, p. 125.

(p. 47, l. 14)   Historical Society of Pennsylvania, Miscellaneous Manuscripts, Chester County, 1684–1847, Robert Parke to Mary Valentine, p. 57, quoted in Williamson, p. 39.

(p. 47, l. 40)   John Winthrop, *A Modell of Christian Charity* in *The Winthrop Papers* (Boston: Massachusetts Historical Society, 1931), quoted in Grimes, p. 29.

(p. 48, l. 18)   Chute, p. 97.

(p. 48, l. 23)   Williamson, p. 6.

(p. 48, l. 37)   *The Statutes at Large: Being a Collection of All the Laws of Virginia, from the First Session of the Legislature in the Year 1619,* ed William Waller Hening (Richmond: 1810–1823), I, 334, quoted in Chute, p. 141.

(p. 49, l. 12)   *The Jefferson Cyclopedia,* II, 841.

(p. 49, l. 16)   Quoted in Arrowood, p. 60.

(p. 50, l. 13)   The *New York Gazette,* February 5, 1761, quoted in Williamson, p. 46.

(p. 50, l. 35)   Williamson, pp. 84–85.

(p. 51, l. 32)   McKinley, pp. 486–87.

(p. 52, l. 36)   *The Records of the Federal Convention of 1787,* ed. Max Farrand, 4 vols. (New Haven: Yale University Press, 1937), I, 423, quoted in Chute, p. 251.

(p. 52, l. 41)   *Ibid.,* II, 210, quoted in Chute, p. 254.

(p. 53, l. 18)   *Ibid.,* II, 244, quoted in Chute, p. 252.

(p. 53, l. 22)   *Ibid.,* I, 431, quoted in Chute, p. 251.

(p. 53, l. 25)   *Ibid.,* II, 31, quoted in Chute, p. 250.

(p. 53, l. 28)   *Ibid.,* I, 48, quoted in Chute, p. 251.

(p. 53, l. 31)   *Ibid.,* I, 299, quoted in Chute, p. 261.

(p. 54, l. 13)   James Madison, *Federalist #10.*

(p. 54, l. 18)   *The Jefferson Cyclopedia,* II, 841.

(p. 54, l. 22)   *Ibid.* (to Dupont De Nemours, 1816).

(p. 54, l. 29)   *Ibid.* (to Chevalier de Onis).

(p. 55, l. 40)   Seymour and Frary, p. 247.

(p. 56, l. 8)   Hofstadter, p. 264.

(p. 56, l. 17)   Pound, p. 15.

(p. 58, l. 35)   Nie, Verba, and Petrocik, p. 87.

(p. 59, l. 4)   *Ibid.,* p. 59.

(p. 59, l. 19)   Flanigan and Zingale, p. 15, Figure 1.1., Estimated Turnout of Eligible Voters in Presidential Elections in the South and Non-South, 1860–1972.

(p. 60, l. 11)   *Ibid.*

(p. 61, l. 4)   Adams, p. 355.

(p. 61, l. 12)   Sherman, p. 352.

(p. 61, l. 27)   Seymour and Frary, p. 261.

(p. 62, l. 35)   Altbach, p. 64.

(p. 64, l. 19)   Flanigan and Zingale, p. 15.
(p. 64, l. 25)   U.S. Government, Department of Commerce, U.S.
                  Bureau of the Census, *Voting and Registration in the
                  Election of November 1972,* p. 5, Table D.

3. THE REFRAINERS: WARTS AND SMILES

(p. 67, l. 22)   See Appendix A for an explanation of the method-
                  ology used in developing the refrainer typology.
                  See Appendix B, Tables 1–6, for presentation of
                  some of the data mentioned in this chapter.
(p. 68, l. 22)   Berelson et al., pp. 307–308.
(p. 73, l. 2)   Poll taken by Mervin D. Field for the *Los Angeles
                  Times,* November 13–24, 1976, of a representative
                  cross-section of California adult public.
(p. 77, Fn.)   Campbell et al., p. 105. *The New York Times,* Novem-
                  ber 16, 1976. *Newsday: LI,* February 22, 1976.
(p. 78, l. 15)   Nie, Verba, and Petrocik, pp. 108–9.
(p. 80, l. 13)   *The Washington Post,* September 17, 1976.
(p. 91, l. 16)   *The New York Times,* September 28, 1976.
(p. 95, l. 2)   Berelson et al., p. 128ff.
(p. 98, l. 30)   Campbell et al., p. 90.

4. QUESTIONS AND SOLUTIONS

(p. 105, l. 14)   William Schneider and Daniel Yergin, "What If
                  They Gave an Election and Nobody Came," *New
                  Times,* October 1, 1976.
(p. 106, l. 23)   Kesey, p. 124.
(p. 107, l. 15)   Locke, p. 42.
(p. 107, l. 37)   Schumpeter, p. 242.
(p. 108, l. 3)   *Ibid.,* p. 243.
(p. 108, l. 18)   *Ibid.,* p. 262.
(p. 109, l. 8)   Beckwith, p. 34.
(p. 110, l. 18)   Berlin, Introduction, p. lviii.
(p. 111, l. 14)   John Stuart Mill, *Considerations on Representative Gov-
                  ernment* (New York: Holt, 1873), cited by Verba and
                  Nie, p. 5.
(p. 111, l. 22)   Berlin, p. lxii.
(p. 113, l. 5)   This is a good place to put to rest some myths about
                  high foreign turnout figures. In the United States,
                  turnout is calculated by taking the number of per-
                  sons who actually voted as a percentage of the
                  estimated civilian voting age population. The U.S.
                  Department of Commerce Bureau of the Census
                  provides the official V.A.P. (voting age population)

figure. This figure includes all people who are old enough to vote, i.e., eighteen and over, and does not exclude those who are legally barred from voting, such as aliens and inmates of penal and mental institutions. It also includes groups who are very unlikely to register and to vote, such as residents of sanitariums, hospital patients, and the mentally and physically incompetent who are not institutionalized. Inclusion of these groups depresses U.S. turnout figures. Estimates of turnout in many other countries are likely to be calculated on a base of the actual eligible voting population, or even just on the numbers of registered voters. In the United States, turnout of registered voters can be as high as 80 percent.

(p. 122, l. 40)   Smolka, p. 25.

SELECTED
BIBLIOGRAPHY

Adams, Henry. *The Education of Henry Adams: An Autobiography.* Boston: Houghton, Mifflin, Company, 1918.

Altbach, Edith Hoshino. *Women in America.* Lexington, Mass.: D.C. Heath & Co., 1974.

Arrowood, Charles Flinn. *Thomas Jefferson and Education in a Republic.* New York: AMS Press, 1970. Reprint from the edition of 1930, New York.

Banfield, Edward C. *The Unheavenly City Revisited.* Boston: Little Brown, 1974.

Banfield, Edward, and James Q. Wilson. "Public Regardingness as a Value Premise in Voting Behavior," *American Political Science Review*, 58 (1974), 876–87.

Beckwith, Burnham P. *Government by Experts.* New York: Exposition Press, 1972.

Berelson, Bernard R., Paul F. Lazarsfeld, and William McPhee. *Voting.* Chicago: University of Chicago Press, 1954.

Berlin, Isaiah. *Four Essays on Liberty.* London: Oxford University Press, 1969.

Bookbinder, Bernie. "Postwatergate Voters," in *Newsday:* Long Island, February 22, 1976.

Butler, David, and Michael Pinto-Duschinsky. *The British General Election of 1970.* London: MacMillan, St. Martin's Press, 1975.

Campbell, Angus, Philip E. Converse, Warren E. Miller, and Donald E. Stokes. *The American Voter.* New York: John Wiley and Sons, Inc., 1960.

Carson, George Barr. *Electoral Practices in the U.S.S.R.* New York: Frederick A. Praeger, 1955.

Chute, Marchette. *The First Liberty*. New York: E.P. Dutton, 1969.

Clausen, Aage R. "Response Validity: Vote Report," *Public Opinion Quarterly*, 32 (Winter 1968–69), 588–606.

Commager, Henry Steele. *The Heritage of America*, ed. Henry Steele Commager and Allan Nevins. Boston: Little, Brown, 1949.

Congressional Quarterly Almanac, vol. XXI. Washington, D.C.: Congressional Quarterly Service, 1965.

Congressional Quarterly Guide to U.S. Elections. Washington, D.C.: Congressional Quarterly, Inc. 1975.

Converse, Philip. "The Nature of Belief Systems in Mass Publics," in *Ideology and Discontent*, ed. David Apter. New York: The Free Press of Glencoe, 1964.

De Vries, Walter, and Lance Tarrance. *The Ticket Splitter*. Grand Rapids: Eerdmans, 1972.

Eidelberg, Paul. *The Philosophy of the American Constitution*. New York: Free Press, 1968.

Elliott, Ward E.Y. *The Rise of Guardian Democracy*. Cambridge, Mass: Harvard University Press, 1974.

Evans, Michael. "Karl Marx and the Concept of Political Participation," in *Participation in Politics*, ed. Geraint Parry. Manchester, England: Manchester University Press, 1972.

The Federalist Papers. Alexander Hamilton, James Madison, John Jay, with an introduction by Clinton Rossiter. New York: New American Library, 1961.

Flanigan, William H., and Nancy H. Zingale. *Political Behavior of the American Electorate*, 3rd ed. Boston: Allyn and Bacon, 1975.

Florinsky, Michael T., ed. *McGraw Hill Encyclopedia of Russia and the Soviet Union*. New York: McGraw Hill, 1961.

Grimes, Alan Pendleton. *American Political Thought*. New York, Chicago, San Francisco, Toronto, London: Holt, Rinehart and Winston, 1960.

Hermens, F.A. "The Dynamics of Proportional Representation," in *Comparative Politics*, ed. Harry Eckstein and David E. Apter. New York: Free Press, 1963.

Hofstadter, Richard, William Miller, and Daniel Aaron. *The United States: The History of a Republic*, 2nd ed. Englewood Cliffs, N.J.: Prentice-Hall, Inc., 1967.

Hollander, Paul. *Soviet and American Society*. New York: Oxford University Press, 1973.

The Jefferson Cyclopedia, vols. I and II, ed. John P. Foley. New York: Russell and Russell, 1967.

Kesey, Ken. *One Flew Over The Cuckoo's Nest*. New York: The Viking Press, 1962.

Key, V. O. *Public Opinion and American Democracy*. New York: Alfred Knopf, 1965.

————. *The Responsible Electorate*. Cambridge: Belknap Press of Harvard University, 1966.

League of Women Voters. "Administrative Obstacles to Voting." Washington, D.C.: League of Women Voters Education Fund, 1972.

Lee, Eugene C. "City Elections: A Statistical Profile," in *The Municipal Year Book 1963*, ed. Orin F. Nolting and David S. Arnold. Chicago: The International City Management Association, 1963.

Lee, Gordon C., ed. *Crusade Against Ignorance: Thomas Jefferson on Education*. Classics in Education No. 6. New York: Teachers' College, Columbia University, 1961.

Locke, John. *Of Civil Government: Second Treatise*, Gateway Edition. Chicago: Henry Regnery Company, 1955.

Mackie, Thomas T., and Richard Rose. *The International Almanac of Electoral History*. New York: Free Press, 1974.

McKinley, Albert Edward. *The Suffrage Franchise in the Thirteen English Colonies in America*. New York: Burt Franklin, 1905.

Merriam, Charles E., and Harold F. Gosnell. *Non-Voting: Causes and Methods of Control.* Chicago: University of Chicago Press, 1924.

Milbrath, Lester. *Political Participation*. Chicago: Rand McNally, 1965.

Mill, John Stuart. *On Liberty*. London: Watts, 1929.

Mill, John Stuart, and Harriet Taylor Mill. *Essays on Sex Equality*. Ed. and with an introductory essay by Alice Rossi. Chicago: University of Chicago Press, 1970.

Morgan, David. *Suffragists and Democrats: The Politics of Woman Suffrage in America*. East Lansing: Michigan State University Press, 1972.

Nie, Norman H., and Kristi Andersen. "Mass Belief Systems Revisited: Political Change and Attitude Structure," *Journal of Politics*, 36 (September 1974), 541–91.

Nie, Norman H., Sidney Verba, and John R. Petrocik. *The Changing American Voter*. Cambridge, Mass: Harvard University Press, 1976.

Ostrogorski, Moisei Iakovlevich. *Democracy and the Organization of Political Parties*. Translated from the French by Frederick Clarke with a preface by the Right Hon. James Bryce. New York, London: Macmillan, 1922, c. 1902.

Petersen, Svend. *A Statistical History of the American Presidential Elections*. New York: Frederick Ungar, 1963.

Pomper, Gerald. *Voter's Choice*. New York: Dodd, Mead and Co., 1975.

Pound, Ezra L. *Jefferson and/or Mussolini*. New York: Stanley Nott, 1935.

Ranney, Austin. *Curing the Mischiefs of Faction*. Berkeley: University of California Press, 1975.

————. *The Doctrine of Responsible Government: Its Origins and Present State*. Urbana: University of Illinois Press, 1954.

———. "Turnout and Representation in Presidential Primary Elections," *American Political Science Review*, 66 (1972), 21–36.

Rose, Richard, ed. *Electoral Behavior: A Comparative Handbook.* New York: Free Press, 1973.

Sait, Edward McChesney. *American Parties and Elections.* New York and London: Century Co., 1927.

Scammon, Richard M. *America Votes: A Handbook of Contemporary American Election Statistics.* Washington, D.C.: Governmental Affairs Institute. Biennial.

Scammon, Richard M., and Ben Wattenberg. *The Real Majority.* New York: Coward, McCann and Geoghegan, 1970.

Schattschneider, E. E. *The Semi Sovereign People.* New York: Holt, Rinehart and Winston, 1960.

Schlesinger, Arthur M., Jr. *Age of Jackson.* Boston: Little, Brown and Co.: 1945.

———. *History of American Presidential Elections.* New York: Chelsea House, 1972.

Schumpeter, Joseph. *Capitalism, Socialism, and Democracy.* New York and London: Harper and Bros., 1947.

Seliger, Martin. *The Liberal Politics of John Locke.* London: George Allen and Unwin, Ltd., 1968.

Seymour, Charles, and Donald P. Frary. *How the World Votes.* Springfield, Mass: C.A. Nichols Co., 1918.

Sherman, William T. *Home Letters of General Sherman*, ed. M.A. DeWolfe Howe. New York: Charles Scribner's Sons, 1909.

Smolka, Richard G. *Election Day Registration: The Minnesota and Wisconsin Experience in 1976.* Washington, D.C.: American Enterprise Institute, 1977.

Steed, Michael. "Participation Through Western Democratic Institutions," in *Participation in Politics*, ed. Geraint Parry. Manchester, England: Manchester University Press, 1972.

Tingsten, Herbert Lars Gustaf. *Political Behavior.* London: P.S. King and Son, Ltd., 1937.

U.S. Government, Bureau of the Census. *Statistical Abstract of the United States:* 1975, 96th ed. Washington, D.C.: 1975.

———. *Voting and Registration in the Election of November 1970.* Series P-20, No. 228, December 1971.

———. *Voting and Registration in the Election of November 1972.* Series P-20, No. 253, October 1973.

———. *Voting and Registration in the Election of November 1974.* Series P-20, No. 293, April 1976.

———. *Projections of the Population of Voting Age for States: November 1976.* Series P-25, No. 626, May 1976.

———. *Voter Participation in November 1976* (advance report). Series P-20, No. 304, December 1976.

Verba, Sidney, and Norman H. Nie. *Participation in America: Political Democracy and Social Equality.* New York: Harper and Row, 1972.

Verba, Sidney, Norman H. Nie, and Jae-On Kim. "The Modes of Democratic Participation: A Cross-National Comparison." Sage Professional Paper, Comparative Politics Series, vol. II, 1970.

Williamson, Chilton. *American Suffrage from Property to Democracy and Social Equality*. New York: Harper and Row, 1972.

Wolin, Sheldon. *The Politics of Vision*. Boston: Little, Brown 1960.

Other References

Caddell, Patrick H., and Albert C. Pierce. "Alienation and Politics: What Is the Electorate Telling Us?" Prepared for Conference on the Electorate and Party Politics, Institute of Politics, Harvard University, June 20–21, 1975.

DeVries, Walter. "American Perceptions of Parties, Institutions and Politicians." Prepared for Conference on the Electorate and Party Politics, Harvard University, June 20–21, 1975.

Field, Mervin D. "Apathy and Disinterest Chief Reason for Low Voting in November Election." Survey prepared for the *Los Angeles Times*, on November 13–24, January 9, 1977.

Hart, Peter D. "Nonvoter Study 1976." Committee for the Study of the American Electorate, Washington, D.C. Material released September 5, 1976.

Teeter, Robert M. "Recent Trends in Voting Behavior." Prepared for Conference on the Electorate and Party Politics, Harvard University, June 20–21, 1975.

———. "Selected Tables from U.S. National Study for 1976 Republican Leadership Conference." Prepared by Republican National Committee Political/Research Divisions. Washington, D.C., March 1975.

APPENDIX A

Technical Explanation of the Refrainer Typology

The categories of refrainers were built in a hierarchical sequence. The guiding rationale for the classifications was that for any one refrainer there would be several possible factors that caused him or her not to vote in 1976 but that some factors should take higher priority than others. The first refrainers to be extracted from the total refrainers and placed in their own group were the bypassed nonvoters. Their almost total ignorance of politics was taken as the primary cause of their nonvoting irrespective of any other piece of evidence to the contrary, including their own explanation for their refraining. Their "know-nothing" characteristic was revealed by the use of two questions (1) "Do you think there are any important differences between the Republican and the Democratic parties (and, if so,) what are they?" and (2) "In general, how often do you usually discuss politics and national affairs with others?" Refrainers who said they "didn't know" if there were any differences between the parties *and* "rarely" discussed politics and national affairs were placed in the bypassed category. However, people who said there were "no differences" between the parties were not put in this category, as their response is not a definite sign of lack of information. Because of the possibility that some of these voters were ignorant of politics through a conscious choice because they were "turned off" by politics, no one was kept in the bypassed group who also possessed a highly cynical attitude about the national government. Cynical voters have a set of beliefs about government and do not belong with the bypassed, who are devoid of any clear political perceptions.

The next group isolated were the refrainers who did not vote because of reasons extraneous to their attitudes about politics, e.g., health, out-of-town, moved, lacked transportation, and so on. Plainly, on election day some people will be too ill to go the polls. A detailed description of how we broke out these refrainers is found in the text, pp. 83–84.

The other "disenfranchised" refrainers were those who volunteered they did not *vote* for one of the following reasons: (1) "no absentee ballot," (2) "couldn't get there—no ride/too far," (3) "out of town/out of state," and (4) "problems with registration/thought I was registered/didn't receive registration card"; or who volunteered they did not *register* for one of the following reasons: (1) "moved/didn't live here long enough," (2) "too late to register/never registered," (3) "didn't know where to register/when to register/registered wrong district," (4) "out of town/out of state/out of country," and (5) "no transportation." As with the healths, an interest screening was used to test these answers. But the test was more severe than for the healths because with some forethought most of these problems could have been overcome. Only if these refrainers said they were "very much interested" in the election even though they didn't vote, were they placed in the *physically disenfranchised* category.

A person's sense of political efficacy was the next possible explanation of the act of refraining which was used in the typology. A feeling of extreme political powerlessness was treated as the governing reason for not voting among the remaining refrainers who felt that way. Consequently, the remaining refrainers who agreed with *all three* of the political efficacy statements were placed in the *politically impotent* category. They agreed that they didn't have "any say about what government does," *and* agreed that "politics and government seems so complicated that a person like me can't really understand what's going on," *and* agreed that "public officials don't care what people like me think." If they answered "don't know," or "disagree" to any of the items, they were not placed in the politically impotent category.

At this point in the sequence, 54 percent of the refrainers had been classified but 46 percent remained undefined. Two further explanations of nonvoting were used to classify as many of the remaining nonvoters as possible: the cross-pressured explanation and the naysayer explanation. All refrainers had been presented with four reasons for not registering or not voting: (1) "I would have (voted/registered) but circumstances prevented me from doing so," (2) "I just wasn't interested enough to (vote/register)," (3) "I purposely didn't (vote/register) because I didn't like the candidates," and (4) "I couldn't make up my mind, so I stayed home." The remaining refrainers who chose the third statement "purposely didn't" as "closest to your own situation" were classified as naysayers, and voters who chose the fourth statement "couldn't make up my mind" were classified as *cross-pressured*.

After these six steps and the resultant categories of refrainers, there were still 35 percent of the nonvoters who had eluded all the definitions of types of nonvoting. They were kept as a single group in the typology. Their characteristics as a group, as found in the subsequent analysis, led to the label, *positive apathetics*.

APPENDIX B

Selected Data from U.S. National Post Election Study of Voters and Nonvoters by Market Opinion Research, November, 1976.

Tables 1–6 show how voters, refrainers (as a group and also as six discrete categories), and vergers answered a range of attitudinal, behavioral, and demographic questions. In *Tables 1* and *2* voters are compared to refrainers. In *Tables 3* and *4* refrainers are compared to each other. In *Tables 5* and *6* vergers are compared to other voters and to all refrainers.

       The Cynicism and Impotency Indices which appear in *Tables 1, 3,* and *5* represent a scale based on the way respondents answered the three political cynicism questions and the three political efficacy questions. For example, in the Cynicism Index "High" shows the percentage of respondents who gave cynical answers to all three political cynicism questions. In the Impotency Index "High" shows the percentage of respondents who answered "I agree" to all three political efficacy questions.

       "Low" shows percentage of respondents who did not give cynical or "I agree" responses to any of the questions.

TABLE 1. ATTITUDINAL AND BEHAVIORAL PROFILES OF VOTERS AND REFRAINERS

	Total 100% (2006)	Voters 100% (1558)	Refrainers 100% (448)	Difference
Total Number of Cases				
Perceived Closeness of Election				
How close did you think the election would be for President—very close, fairly close, or not very close?				
Very close	71	73	63	+10%
Fairly close	18	17	22	− 5
Not very close	7	6	8	− 2
Don't know	4	3	6	− 3
How close did you think the presidential election would be in your state—very close, fairly close, or not very close?				
Very close	45	46	39	+ 7
Fairly close	22	22	23	− 1
Not very close	24	24	25	− 1
Don't know	9	8	13	− 5
Psychological Involvement				
How interested were you in following this year's presidential election—very much, somewhat, or not much interested?				
Very much	64	71	39	+32
Somewhat	24	22	30	− 8
Not much interested	12	7	30	−23
Don't know	1	*	1	− 1
Would you say you personally cared a good deal which candidate won the presidential election or that you didn't care very much who won?				
Cared a good deal	78	84	60	+24
Didn't care	20	15	37	−22
Didn't know	2	1	3	−2

TABLE 1 (Cont'd)

Total Number of Cases	Total 100% (2006)	Voters 100% (1558)	Refrainers 100% (448)	Difference
Political Cynicism How much of the time do you think you can trust the government in Washington to do what is right— just about always, most of the time, or only some of the time?				
Always	6	6	5	− 1
Most of the time	36	38	31	+ 7
Some of the time	52	51	56	− 5
Don't know	6	5	8	− 3
Would you say the government is pretty much run by a few big interests looking out for themselves or that it is run for the benefit of all the people?				
Few big interests	60	58	64	− 6
For benefit of all	26	27	21	+ 6
Don't know	15	15	15	0
Do you think that quite a few of the people running the government are a little crooked, not very many are, or do you think hardly any of them are crooked at all?				
Quite a lot	41	39	44	− 5
Not many	36	37	31	+ 6
Hardly any	16	16	14	+ 2
Don't know	8	7	10	− 3
Cynicism Index				
High	24	23	28	− 5
———	27	26	30	− 4
———	27	29	21	+ 8
Low	20	21	18	+ 3
Not ascertained	2	1	4	− 3

TABLE 1 (Cont'd)

Total Number of Cases	Total 100% (2006)	Voters 100% (1558)	Refrainers 100% (448)	Difference
Political Efficacy				
People like me don't have any say about what the government does.				
Agree	40	37	50	−13
Disagree	55	59	43	+16
Don't know	5	5	8	− 3
Sometimes politics and government seems so complicated that a person like me can't really understand what's going on.				
Agree	64	62	72	−10
Disagree	32	34	23	+11
Don't know	4	4	6	− 2
I don't think public officials care much what people like me think.				
Agree	45	42	55	−13
Disagree	48	52	35	+17
Don't know	7	6	10	− 4
Impotency Index				
High	23	21	30	− 9
———	24	23	30	− 7
———	30	32	24	+ 8
Low	20	23	12	+11
Not Ascertained	2	2	3	− 1
Nonpolitical Attitudes				
Taking all things together how would you say things are for you—would you say you're *very* happy, *pretty* happy, or *not too* happy these days?				
Very happy	30	32	24	+ 8
Pretty happy	50	51	49	+ 2
Not too happy	18	15	26	−11
Don't know	2	2	1	+ 1

TABLE 1 (Cont'd)

Total Number of Cases	Total 100% (2006)	Voters 100% (1558)	Refrainers 100% (448)	Difference
Nonpolitical Attitudes (Cont'd)				
Do you think it's better to plan your life way ahead, or would you say life is too much a matter of luck to plan ahead very far?				
Plan ahead	52	57	37	+20
Too much matter of luck	41	38	54	−16
Don't know	6	5	9	− 4
How often do you usually discuss your personal life with people outside your family—every day, at least once a week, less than once a week, or very rarely?				
Every day	9	9	11	− 2
At least once a week	18	17	22	− 5
Less than once a week	12	12	10	+ 2
Rarely	57	58	54	+ 4
Don't know	5	5	3	+ 2
Past Political Activity: National and Local				
Have you been registered to vote for other elections?				
Yes	0	0	37	0
No/Don't know	0	0	40	0
Registered in 1976	0	0	22	0
Did you vote in the national election two years ago for congressional candidates but not president?				
Yes	55	66	16	+50
No/Never been registered	38	28	77	−49
Don't know	7	6	7	− 1

TABLE 1 (Cont'd)

Total Number of Cases	Total 100% (2006)	Voters 100% (1558)	Refrainers 100% (448)	Difference
Past Political Activity (Cont'd)				
What about local elections —do you always vote in those, do you sometimes miss one, or do you rarely vote, or you never vote?				
Always	47	57	11	+46
Sometimes miss	25	27	16	+11
Rarely	8	6	14	− 8
Never vote/Never been registered	18	8	53	−45
Don't know	2	1	7	− 6
In general, how often do you usually discuss politics and national affairs with others—every day, at least once a week, less than once a week or very rarely?				
Every day	15	17	11	+ 6
At least once a week	32	34	26	+ 8
Less than once a week	15	16	13	+ 3
Rarely	36	32	48	−16
Don't know	2	2	2	0
How often do you usually discuss local community problems with others— every day, at least once a week, less than once a week, or very rarely?				
Every day	16	17	12	+ 5
At least once a week	33	36	25	+11
Less than once a week	16	17	15	+ 2
Rarely	32	28	45	−17
Don't know	2	2	2	0
Have you ever worked with others in your community to try to solve some community problem?				
Yes	41	45	27	+18
No	58	54	72	−18
Don't know	1	1	1	0

TABLE 1 (Cont'd)

Total Number of Cases	Total 100% (2006)	Voters 100% (1558)	Refrainers 100% (448)	Difference
Political Self-Description Generally speaking, do you think of yourself as a Republican, a Democrat, an Independent or what?				
Republican	20	22	12	+10
Democrat	38	39	33	+ 6
Independent	35	34	37	− 3
Other	3	2	5	− 3
Don't know	5	2	12	−10
In politics, do you consider yourself a liberal, a conservative, or a moderate?				
Liberal	20	21	18	+ 3
Conservative	26	27	20	+ 7
Moderate	37	38	34	+ 4
Don't know	17	14	28	−14

TABLE 2. DEMOGRAPHIC PROFILES OF VOTERS AND REFRAINERS

Total Number of Cases	Total 100% (2006)	Voters 100% (1558)	Refrainers 100% (448)	Difference
Region				
East	25	25	25	0
Midwest	27	29	23	+ 6
South	30	28	36	− 8
West	18	18	16	+ 2
Area				
Urban	44	44	45	− 1
Suburban	34	35	31	+ 4
Rural	22	21	25	− 4
Age				
18–24	19	15	33	−18
25–34	22	20	28	− 8
35–44	15	16	9	+ 7
45–54	15	16	11	+ 5
55–64	14	16	8	+ 8
65 and over	15	16	11	+ 5
Education				
Less than high school	21	18	33	−15
High school and technical	40	39	42	− 3
Some college or more	39	43	24	+19
Ethnicity*				
British	24	19	13	+ 6
Irish	19	19	17	+ 2
Italian	5	5	6	− 1
Polish	3	3	3	0
German	17	18	14	+ 4
French	4	4	4	0
Cuban/Spanish-American	3	3	4	− 1
Black/Afro-American	10	9	13	− 4
Eastern European	2	2	1	+ 1
Other	17	17	15	+ 2
Don't know		12	18	− 6
Union Membership				
Union household	27	27	27	0
Non-union household	73	73	73	0

*Multiple responses allowed.

TABLE 2 (Cont'd)

Total Number of Cases	Total 100% (2006)	Voters 100% (1558)	Refrainers 100% (448)	Difference
Religion				
Protestant	55	56	52	+ 4
Roman Catholic	27	28	27	+ 1
Jewish	4	4	3	+ 1
Other/None	13	12	18	− 6
Income				
Under $5,000	17	15	23	− 8
$5,000–$10,000	19	19	22	− 3
$10,000–$15,000	25	24	27	− 3
$15,000–$25,000	29	30	22	+ 8
Over $25,000	10	12	6	+ 6
Race				
White	86	88	81	+ 7
Black	10	9	14	− 5
Spanish American	3	3	4	− 1
Other	1	1	1	0
Sex				
Male	50	50	51	− 1
Female	50	50	49	+ 1
Residency Status 1974-76				
Moved	26	23	39	−16
Changed states	7	6	12	− 6
Less than 50 miles	16	14	22	− 8
More than 50 miles	9	7	15	− 8
No change of address	74	77	61	+16

TABLE 3. ATTITUDINAL AND BEHAVIORAL PROFILES OF TYPES OF REFRAINERS

	Total 100% (448)	By-Passed 100% (60)	Physically Disenfranchised		Politically Impotent 100% (100)	Nay-sayers 100% (28)	Cross-pressured 100% (21)	Positive Apathetics 100% (157)
Total Number of Cases			Health 100% (26)	Moved, Etc. 100% (56)				
Perceived Closeness of Election								
How close did you think the election would be for President—very close, fairly close, or not very close?								
Very close	63	57	68	70	58	66	73	63
Fairly close	22	22	20	22	23	15	16	24
Not very close	8	3	8	8	15	8	6	7
Don't know	6	17	4	0	4	10	4	6
How close did you think the presidential election would be in your state—very close, fairly close, or not very close?								
Very close	39	42	58	36	36	29	48	37
Fairly close	23	23	22	27	17	26	27	24
Not very close	25	11	12	33	32	30	9	27
Don't know	13	24	8	4	16	16	16	11

TABLE 3 (cont'd)

	Total 100% (448)	By-Passed 100% (60)	Physically Disenfranchised		Politically Impotent 100% (100)	Nay-sayers 100% (28)	Cross-pressured 100% (21)	Positive Apathetics 100% (157)
			Health 100% (26)	Moved, Etc. 100% (56)				
Total Number of Cases								
Psychological Involvement								
How interested were you in following this year's presidential election— very much, somewhat, or not much interested?								
Very much	39	30	63*	100*	25	24	21	29
Somewhat	30	24	30	0	29	43	41	40
Not much interested	30	39	7	0	46	33	38	30
Don't know	1	6	0	0	0	0	0	1
Would you say you personally cared a good deal which candidate won the presidential election or that you didn't care very much who won?								
Cared a good deal	60	49	77*	81	57	46	42	60
Didn't care	37	43	23	17	40	54	48	38
Don't know	3	9	0	2	2	0	10	2

*Part of definition

TABLE 3 (cont'd)

	Total 100% (448)	By-Passed 100% (60)	Physically Disenfranchised		Politically Impotent 100% (100)	Nay-sayers 100% (28)	Cross-pressured 100% (21)	Positive Apathetics 100% (157)
Total Number of Cases			Health 100% (26)	Moved, Etc. 100% (56)				
Political Cynicism								
How much of the time do you think you can trust the government in Washington to do what is right —just about always, most of the time, or only some of the time?								
Always	5	4*	4	13	6	4	0	4
Most of the time	31	30	39	33	16	29	48	36
Some of the time	56	30	50	52	78	63	46	54
Don't know	8	36	8	3	0	3	6	6
Would you say the government is pretty much run by a few big interests looking out for themselves or that it is run for the benefit of all the people?								
Few big interests	64	43*	66	59	87	74	66	57
For benefit of all	21	15	30	32	9	12	29	27
Don't know	15	42	4	9	4	15	4	16

*Part of definition

TABLE 3 (cont'd)

	Total 100% (448)	By-Passed 100% (60)	Physically Disenfranchised		Politically Impotent 100% (100)	Nay-sayers 100% (28)	Cross-pressured 100% (21)	Positive Apathetics 100% (157)
			Health 100% (26)	Moved, Etc. 100% (56)				
Total Number of Cases								
Political Cynicism (Cont'd) Do you think that quite a few of the people running the government are a little crooked, not very many are, or do you think hardly any of them are crooked at all?								
Quite a lot	44	16*	51	41	65	50	43	41
Not many	31	31	27	31	23	36	48	35
Hardly any	14	8	18	27	8	14	9	16
Don't know	10	45	4	2	4	0	0	8
Cynicism Index								
High	28	0*	20	27	52	30	18	26
———	30	31	49	23	30	43	39	24
———	21	25	7	25	14	11	23	25
Low	18	23	23	23	4	16	20	23
Not ascertained	4	21	0	2	0	0	0	2

*Part of definition

TABLE 3 (cont'd)

Total Number of Cases	Total 100% (448)	By-Passed 100% (60)	Physically Disenfranchised		Politically Impotent 100% (100)	Nay-sayers 100% (28)	Cross-pressured 100% (21)	Positive Apathetics 100% (157)
			Health 100% (26)	Moved, Etc. 100% (56)				
Political Efficacy								
People like me don't have any say about what the government does.								
Agree	50	48	35	45	100*	45	37	25
Disagree	43	32	46	49	0	51	58	67
Don't know	8	20	20	5	0	4	5	8
Sometimes politics and government seems so complicated that a person like me can't really understand what's going on.								
Agree	72	70	77	66	100*	59	67	59
Disagree	23	14	19	34	0	34	28	34
Don't know	6	15	4	0	0	7	4	7
I don't think public officials care much what people like me think.								
Agree	55	48	65	52	100*	41	34	33
Disagree	35	26	19	45	0	50	52	55
Don't know	10	26	16	3	0	9	14	12

*Part of definition

TABLE 3 (cont'd)

Total Number of Cases	Total 100% (448)	By-Passed 100% (60)	Physically Disenfranchised		Politically Impotent 100% (100)	Nay-sayers 100% (28)	Cross-pressured 100% (21)	Positive Apathetics 100% (157)
			Health 100% (26)	Moved, Etc. 100% (56)				
Impotency Index								
High	30	29	8	29	100*	0*	0	0
	30	29	65	28	0	59	53	37
Low	24	20	23	20	0	26	32	42
	12	8	0	23	0	15	15	18
Not ascertained	3	14	4	0	0	0	0	3
Non-Political Attitudes								
Taking all things together, how would you say things are for you—would you say you're *very* happy, *pretty* happy, or *not too* happy these days?								
Very happy	24	25	8	46	17	22	20	24
Pretty happy	49	41	41	39	48	39	54	59
Not too happy	26	32	51	13	36	34	26	16
Don't know	1	2	0	2	0	6	0	1

*Part of definition

TABLE 3 (cont'd)

Total Number of Cases	Total 100% (448)	Physically Disenfranchised			Politically Impotent 100% (100)	Nay-sayers 100% (28)	Cross-pressured 100% (21)	Positive Apathetics 100% (157)
		By-Passed 100% (60)	Health 100% (26)	Moved, Etc. 100% (56)				
Non-Political Attitudes (Cont'd)								
Do you think it's better to plan your life way ahead, or would you say life is too much a matter of luck to plan ahead very far?								
Plan ahead	37	17	33	45	30	30	33	48
Too much matter of luck	54	54	55	55	66	65	62	44
Don't know	9	29	12	0	4	5	5	8
How often do you usually discuss your personal life with people outside your family—every day, at least once a week, less than once a week, or very rarely								
Every day	11	5	8	15	12	12	15	12
At least once a week	22	16	19	15	20	24	17	28
Less than once a week	10	7	0	12	9	13	19	12
Rarely	54	69	65	57	57	51	49	44
Don't know	3	3	8	0	3	0	0	4

TABLE 3 (cont'd)

| | Total | By-Passed | Physically Disenfranchised | | Politically Impotent | Nay-sayers | Cross-pressured | Positive Apathetics |
			Health	Moved, Etc.				
Total Number of Cases	100% (448)	100% (60)	100% (26)	100% (56)	100% (100)	100% (28)	100% (21)	100% (157)
Past Political Activity: National and Local								
Have you been registered to vote for other elections?								
Yes	37	36	26	51	31	32	40	39
No	40	43	11	25	51	39	46	42
Don't know	1	0	0	0	0	0	0	2
Registered in 1976	22	21	62	24	17	30	14	18
Did you vote in the national election two years ago for congressional candidates but not President?								
Yes	16	10	42	28	5	15	28	15
No	36	37	43	32	38	43	21	36
Don't know	7	10	4	14	6	4	5	6
Never been registered	41	43	11	25	51	39	46	43

TABLE 3 (cont'd)

	Total 100% (448)	By-Passed 100% (60)	Physically Disenfranchised		Politically Impotent 100% (100)	Nay-sayers 100% (28)	Cross-pressured 100% (21)	Positive Apathetics 100% (157)
Total Number of Cases			Health 100% (26)	Moved, Etc. 100% (56)				

Past Political Activity (Cont'd)

What about local elections—do you always vote in those, do you sometimes miss one, or do you rarely vote or do you never vote?

	Total	By-Passed	Health	Moved, Etc.	Politically Impotent	Nay-sayers	Cross-pressured	Positive Apathetics
Always	11	6	19	20	4	20	10	10
Sometimes miss	16	17	27	19	14	15	9	15
Rarely	14	13	31	12	12	14	16	12
Never vote	12	8	4	14	11	8	19	14
Don't know	7	12	8	10	7	4	0	5
Never been registered	41	43	11	25	51	39	46	43

In general, how often do you usually discuss politics and national affairs with others—every day, at least once a week, less than once a week or very rarely?

	Total	By-Passed	Health	Moved, Etc.	Politically Impotent	Nay-sayers	Cross-pressured	Positive Apathetics
Every day	11	0*	12	24	11	14	11	9
At least once a week	26	0	30	36	17	38	30	35
Less than once a week	13	0	15	13	15	15	13	16
Rarely	48	91	39	25	57	33	44	38
Don't know	2	9	4	2	0	0	3	2

*Part of definition

TABLE 3 (cont'd)

Total Number of Cases	Total 100% (448)	By-Passed 100% (60)	Physically Disenfranchised		Politically Impotent 100% (100)	Nay-sayers 100% (28)	Cross-pressured 100% (21)	Positive Apathetics 100% (157)
			Health 100% (26)	Moved, Etc. 100% (56)				

Past Political Activity (Cont'd)

How often do you usually discuss local community problems with others—every day, at least once a week, less than once a week, or very rarely?

	Total	By-Passed	Health	Moved, Etc.	Politically Impotent	Nay-sayers	Cross-pressured	Positive Apathetics
Every day	12	2	15	20	8	14	19	15
At least once a week	25	17	19	32	21	23	14	31
Less than once a week	15	6	8	10	17	14	35	18
Rarely	45	66	54	36	54	45	30	35
Don't know	2	9	4	2	0	3	3	1

Have you ever worked with others in your community to try to solve some community problem?

	Total	By-Passed	Health	Moved, Etc.	Politically Impotent	Nay-sayers	Cross-pressured	Positive Apathetics
Yes	27	13	30	40	18	28	33	32
No	72	82	70	59	81	72	64	67
Don't know	1	5	0	1	1	0	3	1

TABLE 3 (cont'd)

| | Total | By-Passed | Physically Disenfranchised | | Politically Impotent | Nay-sayers | Cross-pressured | Positive Apathetics |
			Health	Moved, Etc.				
Total Number of Cases	100% (448)	100% (60)	100% (26)	100% (56)	100% (100)	100% (28)	100% (21)	100% (157)
Political Self-Description Generally speaking, do you think of yourself as a Republican, a Democrat, an Independent or what?								
Republican	12	12	19	9	14	3	5	14
Democrat	33	26	43	45	40	32	28	27
Independent	37	24	31	40	29	47	48	44
Other	5	4	4	1	7	8	0	5
Don't know	12	34	4	5	10	9	19	9
In politics, do you consider yourself a liberal, a conservative, or a moderate?								
Liberal	18	8	15	20	12	33	31	20
Conservative	20	12	23	17	17	14	9	27
Moderate	34	18	50	46	37	38	35	31
Don't know	28	62	12	17	33	15	25	22

TABLE 4. DEMOGRAPHIC PROFILES OF TYPES OF REFRAINERS

	Total 100% (448)	By-Passed 100% (60)	Physically Disenfranchised		Politically Impotent 100% (100)	Nay-sayers 100% (28)	Cross-pressured 100% (21)	Positive Apathetics 100% (157)
			Health 100% (26)	Moved, Etc. 100% (56)				
Total Number of Cases								
Region								
East	25	14	26	16	26	32	26	29
Midwest	23	33	27	24	20	11	14	23
South	36	47	35	44	40	37	34	28
West	16	6	11	16	14	21	25	20
Area								
Urban	45	45	51	48	45	46	38	43
Suburban	31	30	31	27	28	25	47	32
Rural	25	24	19	26	27	29	14	25
Age								
18–24	33	23	11	29	29	44	35	42
25–34	28	21	7	29	32	28	40	30
35–44	9	7	8	15	12	3	0	8
45–54	11	14	15	9	11	13	10	9
55–64	8	9	27	3	9	3	10	5
65 and over	11	26	31	15	6	8	5	5

TABLE 4 (cont'd)

Total Number of Cases	Total 100% (448)	By-Passed 100% (60)	Physically Disenfranchised		Politically Impotent 100% (100)	Nay-sayers 100% (28)	Cross-pressured 100% (21)	Positive Apathetics 100% (157)
			Health 100% (26)	Moved, Etc. 100% (56)				
Education								
Less than high school	33	50	44	38	32	23	20	28
High school and technical	42	34	48	27	56	43	40	42
Some college or more	24	16	8	35	12	34	40	31
Ethnicity*								
British	13	9	15	13	10	19	14	15
Irish	17	19	23	21	20	12	24	13
Italian	6	0	4	5	6	11	15	6
Polish	3	2	0	5	4	4	0	2
German	14	16	15	20	15	13	14	11
French	4	2	11	2	3	7	5	3
Cuban/Spanish-American	4	5	0	9	3	10	0	3
Black/Afro-American	13	17	12	9	16	9	12	12
Eastern European	1	0	4	0	0	0	0	2
Other	15	12	12	11	15	17	19	19
Don't know	18	26	19	9	20	8	15	19
Union membership								
Union household	27	17	33	33	27	30	21	27
Non-union household	73	83	67	67	73	70	79	73

*Multiple responses allowed

TABLE 4 (cont'd)

	Total 100% (448)	By-Passed 100% (60)	Physically Disenfranchised		Politically Impotent 100% (100)	Nay-sayers 100% (28)	Cross-pressured 100% (21)	Positive Apathetics 100% (157)
Total Number of Cases			Health 100% (26)	Moved, Etc. 100% (56)				
Religion								
Protestant	52	67	52	50	54	44	45	47
Roman Catholic	27	20	45	36	30	19	30	22
Jewish	3	0	0	2	1	11	0	4
Other/none	18	13	3	12	15	26	25	27
Income								
Under $5,000	23	42	59	17	19	13	8	19
$5,000–$10,000	22	29	18	20	18	33	58	19
$10,000–$15,000	27	16	12	32	36	25	25	26
$15,000–$25,000	22	13	12	17	25	17	8	30
Over $25,000	6	0	0	15	3	12	0	6
Race								
White	81	77	79	81	81	81	85	81
Black	14	18	21	10	16	9	15	13
Spanish-American	4	5	0	9	3	10	0	3
Other	1	0	0	0	0	0	0	3
Sex								
Male	51	33	32	46	52	63	60	58
Female	49	67	68	54	48	37	40	42

TABLE 5 (Cont'd)

	Other Voters 100% (1228)	Vergers 100% (330)	Refrainers 100% (448)
Total Number of Cases			

Political Cynicism
How much of the time do
you think you can trust
the government in Wash-
ington to do what is right
—just about always, most
of the time, or only some
of the time?

Always	6	5	5
Most of the time	42	23	31
Some of the time	47	67	56
Don't know	5	5	8

Would you say the govern-
ment is pretty much run
by a few big interests looking out for themselves or
that it is run for the benefit of all the people?

Few big interests	53	77	64
For benefit of all	30	14	21
Don't know	16	9	15

Do you think that quite a
few of the people running
the government are a little
crooked, not very many
are, or do you think hardly
any of them are crooked
at all?

Quite a lot	34	61	44
Not many	41	21	31
Hardly any	17	10	14
Don't know	7	8	10

Cynicism Index

High	17	44	28
———	26	27	30
———	32	17	21
Low	24	11	18
Not ascertained	2	*	4

*Less than one percent

TABLE 5 (Cont'd)

Total Number of Cases	Other Voters 100% (1228)	Vergers 100% (330)	Refrainers 100% (448)
Political Efficacy			
People like me don't have any say about what the government does.			
Agree	20	100*	50
Disagree	74	0	43
Don't know	6	0	8
Sometimes politics and government seems so complicated that a person like me can't really understand what's going on.			
Agree	52	100*	72
Disagree	44	0	23
Don't know	4	0	6
I don't think public officials care much what people like me think.			
Agree	26	100*	55
Disagree	66	0	35
Don't know	8	0	10
Impotency Index			
High	0	100*	30
——	29	0	30
——	40	0	24
Low	29	0	12
Not ascertained	2	0	3
Non-Political Attitudes			
Taking all things together, how would you say things are for you—would you say you're *very* happy, *pretty* happy, or *not too* happy these days?			
Very happy	35	23	24
Pretty happy	51	51	49
Not too happy	13	24	26
Don't know	2	2	1

*Part of definition

TABLE 5 (Cont'd)

Total Number of Cases	Other Voters 100% (1228)	Vergers 100% (330)	Refrainers 100% (448)
Non-Political Attitudes (Cont'd)			
Do you think it's better to plan your life way ahead, or would you say life is too much a matter of luck to plan ahead very far?			
Plan ahead	60	48	37
Too much matter of luck	35	49	54
Don't know	6	4	9
How often do you usually discuss your personal life with people outside your family—every day, at least once a week, less than once a week, or very rarely?			
Every day	9	6	11
At least once a week	18	11	22
Less than once a week	13	10	10
Rarely	55	70	54
Don't know	5	4	3
Past Political Activity: National and Local			
Did you vote in the national election two years ago for congressional candidates but not for President			
Yes	66	65	16
No/Never been registered	28	28	77
Don't know	6	6	7
What about local elections —do you always vote in those, do you sometimes miss one, or do you rarely vote or do you never vote?			
Always	57	58	11
Sometimes miss	27	27	16
Rarely	6	5	14
Never vote/ Never been registered	8	9	53
Don't know	1	0	7

TABLE 5 (Cont'd)

Total Number of Cases	Other Voters 100% (1228)	Vergers 100% (330)	Refrainers 100% (448)
Past Political Activity (Cont'd) In general, how often do you usually discuss politics and national affairs with others—every day, at least once a week, less than once a week, or very rarely?			
Every day	18	13	11
At least once a week	36	25	26
Less than once a week	15	18	13
Rarely	29	44	48
Don't know	2	2	2
How often do you usually discuss local community problems with others— every day, at least once a week, less than once a week, or very rarely?			
Every day	18	15	12
At least once a week	37	30	25
Less than once a week	17	17	15
Rarely	26	37	45
Don't know	2	2	2
Have you ever worked with others in your community to try to solve some community problem?			
Yes	48	34	27
No	51	65	72
Don't know	2	1	1
Political Self-Description Generally speaking, do you think of yourself as a Republican, a Democrat, an Independent or what?			
Republican	23	18	12
Democrat	38	45	33
Independent	34	33	37
Other	3	2	5
Don't know	3	2	12

TABLE 5 (Cont'd)

	Other Voters 100% (1228)	Vergers 100% (330)	Refrainers 100% (448)
Total Number of Cases			

In politics, do you con-
sider yourself a liberal, a
conservative or a
moderate?

	Other Voters	Vergers	Refrainers
Liberal	21	20	18
Conservative	28	24	20
Moderate	38	37	34
Don't know	13	18	28

TABLE 6. DEMOGRAPHIC PROFILES OF VERGERS, REFRAINERS, AND OTHER VOTERS

	Other Voters 100%	Vergers 100%	Refrainers 100%
Total Number of Cases	(1228)	(330)	(448)
Region			
East	25	27	25
Midwest	28	29	23
South	28	29	36
West	19	14	16
Area			
Urban	43	47	45
Suburban	36	32	31
Rural	21	22	25
Age			
18–24	16	12	33
25–34	22	16	28
35–44	17	16	9
45–54	16	15	11
55–64	15	17	8
65 and over	14	24	11
Education			
Less than high school	15	28	33
High school and technical	38	45	42
Some college or more	47	27	24
Ethnicity*			
British	21	14	13
Irish	20	16	17
Italian	5	4	6
Polish	3	5	3
German	18	17	14
French	4	3	4
Cuban/Spanish-American	3	2	4
Black/Afro-American	8	12	13
Eastern European	2	1	1
Other	18	16	15
Don't know	11	16	18
Union Membership			
Union household	27	26	27
Non-union household	73	74	73

*Multiple responses allowed.

TABLE 4 (cont'd)

	Total	By-Passed	Physically Disenfranchised		Politically Impotent	Nay-sayers	Cross-pressured	Positive Apathetics
			Health	Moved, Etc.				
Total Number of Cases	100% (448)	100% (60)	100% (26)	100% (56)	100% (100)	100% (28)	100% (21)	100% (157)
Residency Status 1974–76								
Moved	39	33	24	66	32	33	45	39
Changed states	12	8	4	30	7	14	10	11
Less than 50 miles	22	22	24	25	20	14	24	22
More than 50 miles	15	10	0	41	9	18	14	15
No change of address	61	67	76	34	68	67	55	61

TABLE 5. ATTITUDINAL AND BEHAVIORAL PROFILES OF VERGERS, REFRAINERS, AND OTHER VOTERS

	Other Voters 100%	Vergers 100%	Refrainers 100%
Total Number of Cases	(1228)	(330)	(448)
Perceived Closeness of Election How close did you think the election would be for President—very close, fairly close, or not very close?			
Very close	74	69	57
Fairly close	18	16	22
Not very close	5	9	3
Don't know	3	6	17
How close did you think the presidential election would be in your state—very close, fairly close, or not very close?			
Very close	47	44	39
Fairly close	21	23	23
Not very close	24	24	25
Don't know	7	9	13
Psychological Involvement How interested were you in following this year's presidential election—very much, somewhat, or not much interested?			
Very much	74	60	39
Somewhat	21	26	30
Not much interested	5	13	30
Don't know	*	1	1
Would you say you personally cared a good deal which candidate won the presidential election or that you didn't care very much who won?			
Cared a good deal	85	80	60
Didn't care	14	19	37
Don't know	1	1	3

*Less than one percent.

TABLE 6 (Cont'd)

Total Number of Cases	Other Voters 100% (1228)	Vergers 100% (330)	Refrainers 100% (448)
Religion			
Protestant	56	58	52
Roman Catholic	27	30	27
Jewish	4	3	3
Other/None	13	10	18
Income			
Under $5,000	13	23	23
$5,000–$10,000	17	25	22
$10,000–$15,000	25	23	27
$15,000–$25,000	32	21	22
Over $25,000	13	7	6
Race			
White	89	83	81
Black	8	13	14
Spanish-American	3	2	4
Other	0	1	1
Sex			
Male	50	48	51
Female	50	52	49
Residency status 1974–76			
Moved	23	20	39
Changed states	6	6	12
Less than 50 miles	14	13	22
More than 50 miles	7	5	15
No change of address	77	80	61

INDEX